Beyond Surviving

The Courage to Heal and Lead

"A Journey of Post-Traumatic Growth and Healing After Incest and Childhood Sexual Abuse"

By

Teresa Makeda Stafford

eBook ISBN: 978-1-966931-56-0
Paperback ISBN: 978-1-966931-57-7
Hardback ISBN: 978-1-966931-58-4

Contents

Disclaimer

The content in this book is based on my personal experiences, reflections, and insights. I am not a licensed mental health professional, therapist, or counselor. The information shared is not intended to replace professional mental health treatment, therapy, or counseling. If you are experiencing emotional distress, trauma, or mental health challenges, I strongly encourage you to seek support from a qualified mental health professional.

The stories and perspectives shared are meant to provide encouragement, inspiration, and a sense of connection for those on their own healing journey. However, each person's experience is unique, and what worked for me may not be applicable to everyone. Please prioritize your well-being and seek professional guidance as needed.

If you or someone you know needs support, please reach out to the following resources:

- **National Sexual Assault Hotline**: 1-800-656-HOPE (4673) or visit www.rainn.org

- **National Domestic Violence Hotline**: 1-800-799-SAFE (7233) or text "START" to 88788 or visit www.thehotline.org

- **988 Suicide & Crisis Lifeline**: Call or text 988 or visit www.988lifeline.org

Healing is possible.

A Letter to Survivors

Hey, you. I see you, and I believe you. I know that at times, it might feel like you vs. the world, and no one understands what you are going through. I can remember this feeling: feeling alone and wanting to end it all.

Ashamed of my abuse, ashamed that it was my brother who did all these horrific things to me, ashamed that I allowed others to harm me, ashamed that I turned to sex and other unhealthy habits, ashamed that I was arrested, and ashamed that I consistently thought about ending my life. Hell, I was just ashamed of everything that I did.

Over time, I came to realize that the shame wasn't mine to carry and that my responses to my traumatic experiences were, in fact, normal. Many survivors of sexual abuse, incest, and child sex abuse engage in behavior that gives them a sense of control when they previously did not have any, and others might question their behavior.

I am writing this book for you and for me!

It took me a while to figure things out. It was not always easy, and sometimes I got it wrong. But I NEVER gave up. And you should not either. Together, we got this.

Find your tribe and know that you are worthy. You deserve to look in the mirror and love the person you see. Love the beauty within her and all that she can be. You deserve to set boundaries with people and put your well-being first. You deserve to be loved by others despite what you have been through. You deserve to be able to forgive yourself, even when you are triggered. You deserve an abundant life where you turn your dreams into your reality.

Know that I love you. I am sharing my journey with you, hoping that you will see that YOU can do it, too! I am writing this book to be part of your tribe!

I write this book to share with the reader the complexities of childhood sexual abuse and incest. I will not be sharing the intimate details of my abuse. But more so, how my abuse impacted every aspect of my life. To understand this one does not need the details of what I directly experienced. Just know that throughout the book, I will use terms interchangeably that define my victimization, such as incest, rape, child sexual abuse, abuse, and sexual violence.

This book is dedicated to my daughters Aziah, Taylor, and Brittney. The world is yours, live with purpose and abundantly. And to all the survivors that trusted me to support them on their journey of seeking justice and healing.

Introduction

Our Biography Becomes Our Biology

Every scar tells a story. For many Black girls and women, those stories are written not in ink but in trauma—trauma that etches itself into our bodies, minds, and spirits. Our experiences shape us in unimaginable ways, and when those experiences are steeped in violence, betrayal, and systemic inequities, they begin to manifest in our biology. A closer look at my reality is a truth we often don't say out loud.

The Prevalence of Sexual Violence

- *60% of Black girls experience sexual violence before the age of 18.*
  This devastating figure illustrates the pervasive and intergenerational nature of abuse within marginalized communities. (Black Women's Blueprint, "The Truth Commission on Black Women and Sexual Violence," 2012)

- *Incest is real in the African-American community.* Despite cultural silences and stigma, it is critical to confront and address this reality with sensitivity and support.

The Cycle of Victimization

- Survivors of child sexual abuse are significantly more likely to be re-victimized later in life, perpetuating cycles of harm that go unaddressed in systems meant to protect them.

- *1 in 5 teen girls report physical or sexual abuse by a partner,* demonstrating how early trauma can leave survivors vulnerable to future exploitation. (Futures

Without Violence, Teen Dating Violence Fact Sheet, 2023)

Consequences of Abuse and Inequity

- ○ *Teen pregnancy is often a result of child sex abuse or teen dating violence,* further linking trauma to life-altering outcomes that shape futures.

- ○ *Black girls represent 31% of girls referred to law enforcement and 43% of school-related arrests.* This criminalization deepens the trauma, pushing survivors further away from healing and toward systemic punishment. (Pushout: The Criminalization of Black Girls in Schools, 2018)

Mass Incarceration and its Gendered Racial Impact

- ○ *Black girls account for 32% of all girls in juvenile facilities despite making up just 14% of the population.* These figures underscore the intersection of race, gender, and trauma in shaping outcomes for survivors. (Women's Mass Incarcerations: The Whole Pie 2024)

The Lingering Impact of Child Sexual Assault

- ○ *Survivors are 4 times more likely to develop symptoms of drug abuse*

- ○ *Survivors are 4 times more likely to experience PTSD as adults*

- ○ *Survivors are 3 times more likely to experience a major depressive episode as adults.*

    These data points show that childhood sexual abuse can have a long-term impact on adulthood, especially when the trauma is untreated. (RAINN, 2024)

Chapter 1
Stay Focused: *"You Are Safe"*

Imagine thriving in your career, waking up one morning ready to take on the day, only to be blindsided by an email that drags you back into the depths of your trauma. Then, imagine needing to show up at work, fully present, for people who are navigating their own pain. That was my reality one day in 2010.

I was on my way to work at the County Prosecutor's Office, where I served as the Witness Victim Coordinator when my brother Benny called. *"Did you see Quentin's email?"* he asked, a nervous chuckle trailing his words. *"Quentin's crazy. He's lost his damn mind."*

My heart raced as the weight of his question and laughter set in. Before heading to the office that morning, I checked my email. Quentin's words were paralyzing. It felt as though I had been struck by an 18-wheeler going full speed on a highway. He revealed that our oldest brother had sexually abused him for years. Memories I had worked so hard to bury came flooding back, vivid and relentless; I could barely breathe.

"Why do you think he's crazy?" I asked Benny. His response was blunt and laced with disbelief, *"Do you think he's telling the truth?"* I wanted to scream, *"**HELL YEAH**,"* but standing in the Justice Center, surrounded by colleagues and strangers, I swallowed my words. And I am pretty sure the Deputy Sheriff standing next to me would have responded. The truth was burning inside me, and it was not just Quentin's truth. It was mine, too.

At that moment, I felt torn between two versions of myself: the survivor who had spent years shielding her secrets and the advocate who had dedicated her career to holding space for others.

I had a choice—continue to protect my silence or stand with my brother in solidarity. That choice became my *"Me Too"* moment. With a deep breath, I told Benny, *"He did it to me too."*

For a second, the world seemed to freeze. Benny was quiet before he responded with rapid-fire questions. *"How? When? Why didn't you tell me?"* His voice cracked, and I could feel the weight of his guilt settling over him.

Survivors often fear disbelief, judgment, or rejection when they disclose their abuse. I had carried that fear for decades. Benny's initial response to Quentin was normal. Who wants to believe that a family member or someone they love would cause this type of harm to others?

But now, hearing Benny's anguish, I realize how much trauma affects everyone involved, not just the person harmed. Benny was processing a reality my little brother and I had lived with for years. His pain was fresh, raw. Mine was ancient, layered, and, I thought, under control. But nothing about that day was under control.

"Stay focused; you are safe," I whispered to myself—a mantra I had adopted from years of counseling to help me through moments like this. Those five simple words grounded me, reminding me that while my past shaped me, it did not have to consume me. They were the words that allowed me to refocus on the work I needed to do that morning: meeting with families who had lost loved ones to a serial rapist and murderer. These families deserved my presence, my compassion, and my attention. Somehow, I found the strength to show up for them while my world felt like it was unraveling.

Throughout the day, my phone buzzed nonstop. Benny, overwhelmed and angry, had taken to Facebook to vent about what Quentin and I had shared. I called him immediately, my voice firm but kind: *"This is Quentin's story. This is my story. It's not yours to tell. Please take it down."*

Establishing boundaries is critical for survivors. It is an act of reclaiming power and control, which I've had to learn the hard way. Survivors deserve the right to control the narrative of their own stories. If someone trusts you with their trauma, consider it a profound honor. Hold it gently, as they have given you a piece of them.

Later that evening, I went to see Quentin. I wanted to make sure he was okay, to comfort him as a big sister, but also to reassure myself that he was safe. I brought along one of my sista-friends, Tonae, who is part of my chosen family—my tribe. As I walked into my father's living room, where Quentin sat with our father, I slipped into professional advocate mode with a twist on the big sister thing.

Minutes into our conversation, my father boldly told me he already knew about me. You would have thought someone let off a bomb in the middle of the living room. Did I hear my father tell me he **ALREADY** knew about me? If I could have fought him, kept my career, and not have had any repercussions, I think I would have.

For many years, my main trauma response was to fight. I could feel the rage inside of me surfacing. WTF! How did he know? My then-husband had disclosed my most sacred secrets regarding my abuse to my father. He shared this information, knowing that my father and I didn't have a strong relationship. In counseling, I learned that I saw my father as an extension of my abuse. My rapist shared his name. My abuse worsened after he moved out. When I hear women talk about being a daddy's girl, that was not my reality; I never felt protected by him.

It felt like the air had been sucked out of the room. The man who was supposed to protect me knew about the abuse and said nothing. Years of rage bubbled to the surface. *"You knew, and you didn't say a damn thing to me?"*

I looked at Tonae, then back at my father, and the bomb that went off earlier had landed. I lost it, and it felt so good. I unleashed years of built-up anger on my father. How could a parent be told that their child was sexually abused as a kid and not check in on them? I stood in the middle of the living room screaming at the top of my lungs at my father, questioning his existence as a man and as a father. My father was speechless. I was triggered and went into fight mode with my words. It reminded me of the very volatile outbursts I had growing up.

At the moment, I didn't tap into those tools from counseling to ground myself. Honestly, I am not sure if I was mentally able to. I did not feel safe, and everyone needed to know. If I stayed silent, who would be the voice of that 8-year-old girl who still resided deep inside of me? I felt like Sofia in The Color Purple—"*All my life, I had to fight!*' For once, I wanted someone else to fight for me. It was at this very moment, what I had assumed for years, that I had to be the voice for that 8-year-old girl and the adult me.

A couple of days later, I was upset with myself for losing control. Counseling taught me that I would not always get it right. That I might backslide and make mistakes. Forgiving myself was the best way to move forward. I am human, and making mistakes is part of being human. It is part of the healing journey. Healing isn't linear, and it isn't always pretty. I realized that I was not in a space to engage with my father surrounding this conversation, and it was okay. I did not feel safe, and I had to put boundaries in place to protect myself. The majority of the time, I can handle my triggers.

My father was a trigger that I had not figured out how to handle. I learned how to deal with him over the years by distancing myself. Although he was staying in my rental property, my ex-husband dealt with him. I never imagined that I would hear him tell me that he knew about my abuse, and he never provided me any comfort. He did not check to see if I was okay; he didn't say he believed me or that he was sorry it happened to me. What he did was validate the little girl in me that remained silent. This day was a pivotal point in our relationship. I no longer sought my father's love. He was incapable of giving me what I needed.

I spoke with my cousin Tonya when I finally got home. I shared with her some details of my abuse. I believe it started when I was around eight years old. I don't have a lot of memories of my childhood due to my abuse. My parents were not home often due to work, my mother's illness, and other commitments. My oldest brother was usually left in charge. I was a tomboy, being the only girl with three brothers. So, playing football, wrestling, and roughhousing with my brothers was normal.

The only part that was not normal was the extra touching I experienced. At first, I did not think anything of it. Heck, I was a kid; I thought we were just playing. It was like he was testing me to see if I would say something, and since I didn't, he didn't stop. He was grooming me for what was yet to come. He told me I was his favorite, and he let me play with his stuff that he would not let others touch. He was grooming me into the victim who would stay silent, admire him, and protect him.

As my abuse progressed, I grew to know that it was wrong. The threats, the secrecy, and the feeling in my stomach that was always there let me know that something was not right. Growing up, my parents did not talk with us about our private parts or people touching us inappropriately. By the time I understood what was going on, I was too scared to tell. My fear went beyond just being believed or ashamed. I did not want to be the reason why my mother died.

Around 11 years old, my mother was diagnosed with a rare form of stomach cancer. My parents sat us down in the living room and tried to explain to their children in a manner that we could comprehend that my mother had a terminal illness. She would become a research patient at the National Institute of Health in Bethesda, Maryland, which ultimately meant she would be away from home even more now. I literally died inside, and I cried, and if I can be honest with you, it was not for my mother. Selfishly, I was thinking about myself.

At that point, I knew I could never tell my mother what was happening, and my brother knew this too. My brother turned into a monster. He became even more controlling and dominant, and my abuse went to the next level. He told me that if I told, it would kill our mother. There was no way that I would be the one responsible for my mother's death. I now bore the responsibility of remaining silent to save my mother. It was then that I changed. I was no longer the sweet, sassy little girl people loved. I became this combative, argumentative, violent child that people loathed being around. But, yet, I was still just a child.

Speaking with my cousin brought back memories I had not discussed or considered in years. Remember, I have very vague memories of my childhood due to being sexually abused. I blocked a lot out. A memory I blocked out can come rushing to the forefront at any moment. On this night, so many of those memories were at the forefront of my mind. I could barely focus. People kept calling, wanting to understand how this could have happened, asking why I did not say anything, and trying to be a liaison between my abuser and me.

I had to keep chanting to myself, *"Stay focused; you are safe."* But was I truly safe? My perpetrator was just outed publicly. What did he have to lose? He was still a violent individual. The trope of the strong Black woman kicked in. I presented to everyone that I was handling everything okay. For the next several days, I lived in a constant state of fear for my safety, paranoia, and hypervigilance.

My Aunt Bonnie and her husband, Uncle Bruce, were two of my favorite people. My mother and her sister, both married men named Bruce. My Aunt and Uncle never knew that they provided me with safety by spending time with them in Chicago while growing up. I would spend a couple of weeks with them during the summer months. I remember begging them to let me stay with them permanently, and my parents seriously considered it with my mother's illness. At the last moment, my mother changed her mind.

Aunt Bonnie tried to be the peacemaker when the family learned of our abuse. She was the main person trying to be the liaison between my rapist and me. As a result, our relationship was never the same. People who protected my abuser became triggers for me, and their role in my life was repositioned. I found myself doing this consistently over the years.

The day I received the email from Quentin was one of the longest days of my life in years. There was no more hiding my abuse within my small circle of friends and counselors I engaged with over the years. For a moment, I felt like I did not have any control. Not having control is a horrible feeling for survivors of sexual violence. I felt like I was always trying to survive.

People who experience trauma often encounter triggers—those subtle (or not-so-subtle) reminders of a past hurt. Triggers can be anything: a familiar scent, a certain sound, or even an unexpected thought that drags you back into a place of pain. For some, these moments can feel paralyzing, pulling them into avoidance behaviors that isolate them from others and deepen feelings of depression or a need to isolate.

For me, triggers were like ambushes. My body would react before my mind could catch up—heart racing, sweaty armpits, a desperate urge to escape. Sometimes, I'd shut down entirely: ghosting people, becoming defensive, or retreating mentally, even while physically present. These reactions were not always conscious choices; they were my body's way of trying to protect me from harm, whether the threat was real or imagined.

Understanding my triggers became crucial for my healing. Instead of fearing them, I had to get curious about them. Why did certain things set me off? Why did I feel unsafe in moments that seemed harmless to others? Counseling became my safe space to unpack these questions and examine my responses with honesty and compassion. Honestly, this was a hard part of counseling to engage in, and I would stop at times because it was hard work.

Ultimately, my desire for something different eventually allowed me to do the hard work. By identifying my triggers, I began to regain control—not over the world around me, but over how I responded to it. Each insight felt like reclaiming a piece of myself that trauma had stolen.

Through counseling and introspection, I started recognizing the patterns that shaped my reactions and building the tools to navigate those moments with strength and clarity. Understanding my triggers was not just about surviving—it was about learning to live fully again. Some of my triggers include:

- People who have a relationship with my abuser. I have always seen individuals who maintain a relationship with my abuser as problematic. This was even before my abuse was disclosed publicly. He was a horrible human. How could you be friends or engage with him after learning what he did to me? Do you even believe it happened? Are you like him? I would instantly feel uncomfortable and unsafe when I realized that someone I knew or trusted was still in some type of relationship with him, regardless of learning that he was a rapist.

- People who, over the years, have learned about the abuse but have the audacity to ask me questions about him. No, the f^%K I haven't seen him; I don't know what he is doing or where he lives. And, the majority of the time it was family members asking me these questions.

- Men who exert their power and lean into toxic masculinity and misogynistic behavior.

- Hugs and specific touches, especially when someone would sneak up behind me.

- Liars.

- When someone would yell or raise their voice towards me.

Chapter Activities – Understanding Triggers

What Are Triggers in the Context of Trauma?

Triggers are stimuli, such as situations, words, sounds, smells, or memories, that remind individuals of past traumatic experiences, causing emotional or physical distress. They can activate the brain's fight, flight or freeze response, even when there is no immediate danger, as the body reacts as if the trauma is happening again. My father's acknowledgment of knowing about my abuse and not saying anything to me was a trigger on top of learning about my brother's abuse.

Keys Aspects of Triggers in Trauma:

1. Unpredictable and Individualized:

    - Triggers vary greatly from person to person. A specific song, a certain scent, or even a tone of voice might feel harmless to some but overwhelming to others based on their trauma history.

2. Emotional Responses:

   - Triggers often evoke strong emotions such as fear, sadness, anger, shame, or guilt. These responses can feel disproportionate to the current situation but are deeply tied to past trauma.

3. Physical Symptoms:

   - Experiencing a trigger can lead to physiological reactions such as sweating, rapid heartbeat, trembling, nausea, or shortness of breath.

4. Implicit Memory Activation:

   - Triggers can bring up implicit memories, sensations, or emotions associated with the trauma that might not be tied to a clear narrative or explicit memory.

5. Disconnection from the Present Moment:

   - For many, triggers can cause dissociation, making them feel as though they are reliving the trauma or are detached from their current surroundings.

Understanding triggers is crucial in trauma recovery. Recognizing and managing them helps individuals regain a sense of control and safety, breaking the cycle of reactive responses and facilitating healing. Take a moment and think about times that you have felt unsafe or had profound memories of your traumatic experiences. What was going through your mind? What were you doing? What did you see or smell? Who was present? I found it helpful to keep a small journal with me to write down when I was triggered to see if I could identify a pattern. You can even use your phone to keep a digital journal if it's safe. Once you can identify your triggers, you are better able to manage them. Notice, I didn't say prevent them. Trauma is connected to the body; it lives within the body. Therefore, it was paramount that I paid attention to how my body responded to my triggers to better manage them.

Trigger	Body's response	Connection to Trauma
Example: Unwanted hugs or touches	Example: My body would freeze, or I would disconnect from the situation	Example: I would often freeze and just disconnect while being abused.

Here's a list of practical strategies to help manage and navigate triggers when they arise. If you notice you are having triggers often or they are debilitating, please seek professional support from a licensed counselor.

1. Grounding Techniques

Grounding techniques help anchor you to the present moment, redirecting your focus away from the trigger.

5-4-3-2-1 Technique:

- Identify:
    - 5 things you can see
    - 4 things you can touch
    - 3 things you can hear
    - 2 things you can smell
    - 1 thing you can taste

Deep Breathing:

Inhale deeply through your nose for 4 seconds, hold for 4 seconds, and exhale through your mouth for 6 seconds.

Engage Your Senses:

Carry a small sensory item, like a smooth stone, scented lotion, or gum, to focus on tactile, olfactory, or taste sensations.

2. Positive Self-Talk and Affirmations

Replace distressing thoughts with empowering ones. Examples include:

- "This feeling will pass."
- "I am safe right now."

- "I've survived this before; I can handle it again."

3. Create a Safe Space

Designate a physical or mental space that brings you comfort:

- Physical Space: Go to a location where you feel secure, such as a favorite room or a quiet park.

- Mental Space: Visualize a place where you feel safe and calm. Use details like the color of the sky, the sound of waves, the smell of fresh grass, or the sound of your favorite song.

4. Practice Mindfulness

Mindfulness helps you stay present and observe your thoughts without judgment.

- Meditation Apps: Use apps for guided meditations.

- Focus on Your Breath: Count your breaths or repeat a calming word (e.g., "Peace" or "Safe").

- Observe Without Reacting: Note your feelings and sensations with phrases like "I notice.."

5. Set Boundaries

Empower yourself by saying "no" or excusing yourself from triggering situations:

- Use phrases like, "I need a moment" or "I'm not ready to discuss this."

- Limit interactions with people who disregard your emotional boundaries.

6. Seek Support

Don't be afraid to lean on others when needed:

- Talk to a trusted friend or family member.

- Join a support group for survivors of trauma.

- Reach out to a therapist for professional guidance.

7. Plan Ahead by Creating a Safety Plan

Prepare for situations where you might encounter triggers:

- Create a list of coping strategies you can use in real-time.

- Develop an exit strategy for overwhelming situations.

- Inform trusted individuals about your needs so they can offer support if needed.

Chapter 2
Juvenile Delinquent:
That's what they called me!

The trauma I faced at a young age ignited a storm of rage inside me, a seething anger that lurked, waiting for any excuse to explode. Fighting became my outlet, my weapon, and my defense. I fought constantly, and I was good at it—fighting boys, girls, anyone who dared me. Each blow, each victory, fueled a sense of power and control that I could only find in those moments. Fighting was the one place I felt invincible.

Oddly enough, fighting allowed me to create a version of myself that seemed strong, someone untouchable, someone who could never be hurt. This hardened persona became my shield, a way to mask the truth of my vulnerability. Behind every punch thrown and every win, I was hiding a reality I was not ready to face.

I started *masking* at a young age. Masking for me meant not being my authentic self, hiding and suppressing my reality in an effort to gain greater social acceptance and just to literally survive daily. I was masterful at it, creating a façade of strength that was both my protection and my prison. Even now, I sometimes catch myself slipping back into that mask, and I remind myself that healing isn't a destination—it's a lifelong journey.

Unknowingly, I embraced the trope of the '*Strong Black Woman*' long before I even understood its weight. By thirteen, I had internalized that strength was survival, that what didn't kill me was supposed to make me stronger. I watched my mother embody this resilience: even as illness wore her down, she never stopped. It was as if her strength was her legacy, passed to her from my grandmother and, in turn, down to me–It's generational. I was built for this shit! I repeatedly heard this from Black people in my life, the Black church, the media, and every corner of society. Seriously, I wasn't built for this shit. I was experiencing the impact of cultural and historical trauma.

Cultural and historical trauma refers to the collective emotional and psychological wounds passed down through generations within a community as a result of systemic oppression, violence, and marginalization. For Black women, this trauma is deeply intertwined with the legacy of slavery, racism, sexism, and other forms of systemic inequities that continue to impact their lives today.

Cultural and historical trauma explains why so many Black girls and women stay silent about their pain. We live in a world where we are often disbelieved, unprotected, deemed unworthy, or unsupported. Leaning into this image of the strong Black woman became a survival strategy for me, a shield to carry when I felt unprotected, devalued, or internalized the negativity others projected onto me. Masking was my way of navigating a world that had little room for my vulnerability.

In doing so, I sacrificed pieces of myself. The softness, the femininity that others might expect or celebrate in someone else, became buried. It was almost as if, to survive, I had to relinquish parts of my own womanhood. Both dominant culture and, at times, Black culture itself had little space for my femininity that needed protecting, too. And so, I hid it, becoming what the world expected: a pillar of strength, a fortress. But beneath that exterior, I was holding back years of pain.

As I moved through my healing process, I learned that fighting was my way of protecting myself from anyone interested in harming me and appearing strong enough to handle anything. If they saw me as this tough girl, they wouldn't try me. The logic of a 13-year-old is almost laughable, but that's how survival looked to me then.

As a professional who works in the criminal justice system, I constantly remind other professionals that our youth just do not wake up and think, *"Today's the day that I'm going to fight or act out."* Their continuous negative behavior is typically a coping mechanism for something negative they have experienced. Grace by the professionals was not often extended to youth in the juvenile justice system who looked like me, especially Black girls. My trauma response was seen as criminal.

I attended Whitney Young Junior High School, the Cleveland public school for gifted and talented students who were in the major work program. I barely made it to Whitney Young. I remember the teacher that I had for 5th and 6th grade would point out that I wasn't major work material. I would not finish work to the best of my capabilities, quickly lose focus in class or have a hard time digesting information. How could I function at school to my fullest capabilities when I'm dealing with being abused?

Imagine being sexually violated in the middle of the night or right before school and then being expected to perform at your best in class. My brain simply wouldn't allow it. I couldn't focus. It was like my brain was racing all over the place, and I couldn't quiet it down. But instead of asking what happened to spark this change in my school performance, I was told I wasn't enough. Being sexually abused already made me question my worth now I have adults in my life confirming my thoughts. This theme of not being worthy had infiltrated every aspect of my life as a survivor and even later as a professional working in the anti-violence field.

In junior high school, my abuse had progressed, and I did not see a way out. Remember, telling my mother was not an option. I was severely depressed but functioning. I hated life. I maneuvered through life in a constant state of hypervigilance. I was extremely sensitive to my surroundings, always on alert to any hidden or perceived dangers.

Even though I told no one at this time what was going on, my paranoia had me thinking differently. I am pretty sure this contributed to my willingness to fight others so freely. Trauma will have you doing things that contradict who you are as a person. Counseling eventually gave me tools to understand my trauma responses and why they manifested. This understanding eventually allowed me to give myself the grace that others would not.

In junior high school, I stopped taking care of my hygiene and really did not care how I looked. I went to school a funky mess. Students would talk about me, and if I heard them, I would fight them. Hell, I knew I stank. It was my way of protecting myself. I kept creating these methods of protection and survival because, again, telling someone never seemed an option.

By this time, I was assaulted by another person. While visiting my aunt in Chicago, her best friend's son raped me while we were supposed to be in the basement watching television. He was older and kept pushing himself on me. Instead of pushing him off, I froze. That summer was my last trip to spend time with my Aunt and Uncle in Chicago. Chicago was the one place I felt safe, and I no longer had my safe landing.

I felt like a walking target for people to take advantage of at their leisure. How could this happen to me again? What am I doing that makes people want to harm me? I started internalizing my victimization in a new way. People abusing me had to be my fault. Who the hell is sexually assaulted by different people in such a short time span?

I kept taking my anger out on others. One day, my older brothers met me after school at Whitney Young. A girl walked past me, and in my mind, she looked at me like she had a problem. I ran up to her and started fighting her. I had to show my abuser that I was tough even though the abuse was starting to happen less. She received a substantial injury during the fight and didn't deserve what happened.

The principal wanted to kick me out for my behavior, but my grades were good, and people assumed I was acting out because of my mother's illness. By this time, my parents had separated. Everyone had a reason for my behavior, but no one seemed interested in learning the truth; they never asked, they assumed. Adults assuming they knew what was wrong became common over the next couple of years, which further influenced my silence.

My brother stopped sexually abusing me before I started high school. Our relationship was strange. While he caused so much harm to me, he protected me from others. He became one of my biggest protectors and enemies at the same time. Was this his way of trying to apologize for hurting me? Or was he playing mind games with me? I was so confused and did not have a positive release from my trauma. Survivors of incest may experience high levels of secrecy, betrayal, powerlessness, guilt, conflicted loyalty, fear of reprisal, and self-blame/shame. I was experiencing all of this, and it became overwhelming at times.

I had to find an outlet. My brain never shut down. I played sports and tried to stay busy, but it was not enough. I was angry and kept taking it out on others. Because I was in major work, I was supposed to be bussed to the West side of Cleveland to attend John Marshall High School. My mother decided not to bus me and pulled me from the program. For the first time, I attended school with my two older brothers at John F. Kennedy High School. It was one of the biggest mistakes my mother made unknowingly. I entered high school at 13 years old and took masking to a whole new level. I played all the sports and was pretty good. My classes were pretty easy since I was in regular classes. Much of my classwork in 9th grade was a repeat of the 8th grade. I cut classes,

19

and my coaches covered for me a lot. I started smoking weed, drinking, and having sex to numb my pain.

I was a young freshman at 13 years old who had experienced so much and was longing for a sense of belonging—A purpose. I found what I was looking for by joining a gang. The gang gave me a sense of belonging, protection, and love that I wasn't getting at home. I don't remember my parents telling me they loved me, that I was pretty, or even giving me hugs. The gang gave me this. They gave me what I thought was love. I started running away from home. My relationship with my mother was a ticking time bomb. We fought constantly. Even though I had a warm bed at home, I chose to sleep in cars and other unsafe conditions that felt safer than sleeping at home.

Although the abuse had ended, its presence lingered like a shadow that refused to fade. Living in the same house, sleeping in the same bed where I had been violated, felt like a never-ending horror story. Every creak of the stairs, every familiar smell, every glance at the walls held echoes of what had happened. No matter how much I tried, I could not escape these memories.

The sexual abuse did not just harm me. It fundamentally changed me. I felt like a piece of myself had been stolen— something irreplaceable. I was not just mourning what had happened. I was mourning what *could have been*. I was grieving the version of me that might have existed if those experiences had not fractured my sense of safety and self. I was lost, fumbling in the darkness for a version of myself that no longer existed.

But my grief was complicated. I was not just mourning the loss of my innocence or my sense of security; I was mourning the loss of someone who was a part of my life. My abuser wasn't a stranger; he was someone I grew up with, someone I shared a home with. That duality was almost unbearable: grieving the harm while grappling with the loss of a person I had been connected to in ways I could not easily untangle. Joining the gang became my outlet, something I could focus on.

Professionally and through counseling, I learned that joining a gang made sense to my 13-year-old trauma brain. Girls in gangs often have serious histories of sexual and physical abuse. In one study, researchers found that 62 percent of the girl gang members had been sexually abused or assaulted in their lifetime; three-fourths of the girls (and more than half of the boys) reported suffering lifetime physical abuse.[1] Gangs can provide a sense of identity, especially for those who feel disconnected from family or society. I joined the gang because I was looking for a sense of belonging, companionship, and validation.

The fighting would eventually catch up with me during my freshman year. I was at my high school Valentine's dance with my boyfriend and the rest of the gang. We had a co-dependent relationship. He was my protector, but our relationship was not the healthiest; this would become a common theme with men in my life.

At the dance, a girl that I knew kept bumping into me while I was dancing. As you may have guessed, this led to a fight. The fight ended the dance and continued on the streets. So much happened that night; instead of being scared, I was on an adrenaline high. I left with the rest of the gang, but not before the principal told me not to return to school. I was being expelled. I was able to hide this from my mother for a couple of weeks. She was away in Maryland at the National Institute of Health, and my father was too busy to be fully present in his kids' lives. For a week, I left every morning

---

[1] https://www.ojp.gov/sites/g/files/xyckuh241/files/media/document/243473-Chapter9.pdf

as though I was going to school to hang out with the gang at a house that we could access.

The crazy thing was when my mother returned home. She did not know that I was kicked out of school immediately. As a parent, I am baffled about the lack of communication from the school to my parents. They must have assumed that I would tell my parents that I got kicked out of school, right?

After drinking and smoking weed all day at this house we had access to, we caught the bus back to the school in time for dismissal. We got into a fight on the bus with a grown man who was overly flirtatious with my friend and me. During the fight, my right hand was hit with a cane, causing a big cut on my thumb. I was bleeding all over the place. The bus driver called the police, and we ran to the high school. My plan was to sneak into the school and take care of my hand in the locker room. We ran into my boyfriend in the school parking lot, and we started arguing. A few minutes later, I was surrounded by the police and arrested. I later learned that the man we fought had sickle cell and had a seizure. He was rushed to the hospital.

I was taken to the 4th District police station before being transported to the juvenile detention center. While at the 4th district police department, my parents had the opportunity to come to get me but refused, even though they bailed out my brothers when they were arrested as juveniles. I remember sitting in the holding cell at the 4th district for what seems like forever. I was eventually transferred to the juvenile detention center.

As a survivor of sexual abuse, the whole intake process was triggering. Upon intake at the detention center, the officer, a stranger, patted me down, feeling all over my body to ensure that I did not have any contraband. I understood the purpose, but it felt like my body was being violated all over again, and I froze. I did not respond to the officer's directions and was immediately seen as a problem. I could not move. I was just thrown back into the times when my brother would have his way and touch my body.

The four of us were arrested that day and charged with aggravated robbery and assault. When I went in front of the judge, I was released to my parents. I got into it with my parents and screamed that I just wanted to die. They drove me right to Windsor Laurelwood Behavioral Health Center, where I was placed on suicide watch for three days.

I spoke with a counselor and told them I was just mad because my parents did not pick me up immediately upon my arrest. I have had suicidal thoughts throughout the years, and this honestly was not one of them. I was at Laurelwood for three days, and again, everyone assumed I was acting out because of my mother's health and my parent's separation. No one seemed to be concerned with the truth because no one asked. So, I continued to remain silent about my abuse.

When I went back to court, I was placed in Cleveland Christian Home, an intensive care residential treatment facility. To this day, I never understood why the court removed me from my home. They did not know about my abuse. Why didn't I get a chance to engage with a counselor in outpatient treatment? Everyone's response to my behavior seemed so drastic without anyone knowing the truth. Imagine if they knew the truth, where would they send me? I didn't last long at the facility. The Cleveland Christian Home housed girls from all over the inner city of Cleveland and Cuyahoga County.

I was seen as the suburban girl since I did not live in what was considered the 'hood.' I was allowed to attend a CAVS basketball game with my high school coach. When I returned, I noticed that someone had been looking through my personal items in my room.

I went into the common area and saw a girl wearing my sweater. I tried to tell the staff, but they disregarded me. My brother Benny told me not to let anyone punk me, or they would keep bothering me. If I did not handle things with her, it would set up a dynamic where the others saw me as weak and would take advantage of me.

I did what I knew best and fought the girl for stealing my items. As a result, I was returned to the juvenile detention center and was held there until my trial. From my personal experience and later my professional experiences, I noticed that most criminal justice professionals do not understand the dynamics that I was presented with and why I felt I had to fight to further protect myself or get taken advantage of in the group home. Again, I found myself making decisions based on survival.

Judge Betty J. Ruben was the assigned judge. During one of my pretrial hearings, she made me write a paper on sickle cell due to the victim in the case diagnosis. At my next pretrial hearing, I presented her with a thoroughly researched paper, which only seemed to aggravate her. I am pretty sure she only saw me through the eyes of the professionals who submitted reports regarding my negative behavior as a delinquent. I do not recall actively participating in the court process. I do remember her asking me what I learned from my research.

Sarcastically, I let her know that a grown man with sickle cell should not be flirting with kids on a bus. I felt that Judge Ruben saw me as this unruly black girl who was acting out and rebelling against authority, and I presented as such. An attorney from my church represented me, and under their direction, I pled guilty to the charges. I assumed that I would be sent home on probation like the other female in my case. However, I was declared a juvenile delinquent by the State of Ohio and sentenced to the Scioto Juvenile Correctional Facility. Yes, I fought a lot, but this was my first and only arrest.

I had mixed feelings about my sentencing. Part of me was relieved. I would not have to live in the house with my abuser for a whole year. I did not sleep much for fear of him coming into my room at night. I might actually be able to sleep peacefully in jail! By the end of my sentence, he should be on his way to college and living on campus. Although the abuse had stopped, I feared it would start back, and our relationship became volatile. I hated him with every fiber in my body, and others would act like he was this great human being.

Being declared a juvenile delinquent made it seem as though I was the problem all along. Well, at least for the next year, I did not have to deal with him. You might be thinking, Teresa, why didn't you just tell someone? I still had in the back of my mind that my mother might die if I told her. And to me, I couldn't trust these folks. They were putting me in handcuffs, locking me in a cell, and telling me I was the problem. Honestly, how could I trust a system that saw me as a criminal? Would they even believe me?

The educational and criminal justice systems often implement punitive responses to how survivors of child sexual abuse respond to their trauma, specifically survivors of color. Pushout: *The Criminalization of Black Girls in Schools* by Monique Morris highlights the need for school systems to develop restorative practices instead of pushing girls out of school into unhealthy, unstable, and unsafe environments. Imagine if I had early intervention instead of being constantly suspended from school and how things might have turned out differently.

While working in the sexual violence field, I trained juvenile justice practitioners within the juvenile justice system. During a human trafficking training session with prosecutors, public defenders, judges, and Guardian ad Litem, before I spoke, the Judge who oversaw the specialized docket for human training told the attendees that these kids were mean, angry, and often disrespectful. I stood there listening to her while the attendees nodded their heads in agreement. I looked over at my team of advocates, who looked uncomfortable. My underarm pits started sweating, and my stomach started turning.

I knew I could not stand there and not respond to the message the attendees were receiving. When it was my turn, I told them about a young lady who experienced sexual abuse for years and other traumas. I told them how, after one arrest for fighting, she ended up in the criminal justice system and sentenced to juvenile prison. I shared with them some other details to disclose that I am that girl; when I matriculated through the juvenile justice system, I was more than positive that I had an attitude. That I am sure I came off as disrespectful. But considering the circumstances and my life filled with trauma, the professionals should understand that it is not personal. Instead, they have an opportunity to dig deeper to gain an understanding of why.

Today, there is so much research regarding the Sexual Abuse to Prison Pipeline, which describes the pathways of gender-based violence that led girls into the juvenile justice system as a direct result of their sexual victimization[2]. In 2015, the Human Rights Project for Girls released the report The Sexual Abuse to Prison Pipeline: The Girls Story. I received this report as the Senior Director of Victim Advocacy and Outreach while working at the local rape crisis center. I started reading the report at work and quickly decided this was something I needed to read at home in private. It was a difficult read because I was that report.

Even though I have acknowledged my trauma, reading that report left me with so many emotions. I was immediately reminded that my healing is a lifelong journey. That what happened to me 27

---

[2] Rebecca Epstein, Lindsay Rosenthal, Malika Saada Saar, & Yasmin Vafa, Georgetown Law Center on Poverty and Inequality, Ms. Foundation for Women & Rights4Girls, The Sexual Abuse to Prison Pipeline: The Girls' Story (2015).

years ago can come rushing back to the surface at any given moment. I was at first saddened that the report had to be created to explain why so many girls are engaging with the criminal justice system, and then those feelings were replaced with anger. I was pissed off that we are still using the criminal justice system to respond to the needs of girls who have been victimized.

While in Scioto Village, I didn't have many problems. I was able to catch up with my schoolwork, maintained good grades, and received little to no infractions. The crazy thing is that I actually flourished there. And no, it was not because I had structure. I did not have to see or breathe the same air as my rapist. My brain was not constantly triggered to fight or flight. My mother would visit as often as she could when she was not sick. At some point, my mother got sicker than normal, and no one would tell me what was going on. It was the one time that I had one of my violent outbursts. I was placed in lock-up. I did not stay there long at all, maybe 30 minutes. They just wanted me to calm down and then assisted with getting me information about my mother. I felt seen and heard. They listened to me and responded.

As my release date approached, my mother was working to identify a high school for me to attend. I could not return to my old high school. My mother wanted to send me to boarding school but couldn't afford it alone, and my father refused to assist. My mother was able to enroll me in Martin Luther King Law and Public Service School (LPS) in the Hough community with the assistance of her friend, Mr. Jones, the principal.

Upon returning home, I was placed on probation and threatened to return to Scioto Village if I got into any trouble. My abuser was attending Cleveland State University and lived on campus. I could go home to peace. Attending a new school in a community across town came with many challenges. I was the new girl that didn't live in the community and I knew no one.

It was sort of a fresh start. That was until some of the girls saw me as a threat. All I could do was ignore them. I didn't want to get locked up again. My probation officer visited me at school, which only made things worse. My paranoia kicked it. Did people really know that I was locked up? I always seemed to be holding a secret of some sort. My brother Benny typically would pick me up from school. I had to catch several buses home when he didn't pick me up.

One day, on the way to the bus stop, the girl I was having trouble with started talking loudly and harassing me. I knew what this meant. I couldn't risk my freedom again, but this was a fight I couldn't prevent. There was no walking back to the school. I was surrounded by other students who had circled the other girl and me. A fight ensued. Something inside of me snapped during the fight. I knew I was going back to Scioto Village. I was so angry. I remember having the girl in a headlock before someone stepped in and got me off of her.

When I made it home, I went straight to Benny, arguing that it was all his fault for not picking me up. I remember him pointing to my arm, asking if it hurt. This whole time, I didn't realize that she bit my left bicep area when I had her in the headlock. My arm was swollen, the flesh was exposed, and bleeding. I have permanent teeth marks to this day on my arm. Benny told my mother, and being the nurse that she was, she cleaned me up before taking me to the hospital. I told her what had happened, and I think she actually believed me. My mother took me to school the next day. The principal was waiting for us when we arrived. I told him what had happened, and he believed me. Mr. Jones knew that I might have to fight to prove myself and that he would not contact my probation officer. I felt heard and supported. Maybe, just maybe, I could finally tell someone what happened to me. Mr. Jones showed me that adults have the power to make sound decisions even when they might go against policies that are in place.

Chapter Activities: Trauma Responses

Trauma responses are the ways our minds and bodies react to overwhelming events or experiences that threaten our sense of safety, stability, or well-being. These responses are often automatic, deeply rooted in survival mechanisms, and shaped by our individual experiences, biology, and environment.

Trauma responses are natural and normal reactions to abnormal circumstances, but when unresolved, they can persist and interfere with daily life, relationships, and mental health.

Types of Trauma Responses

1. Fight

    - Reacting to perceived danger with aggression, anger, or attempts to assert control.

    - Example behaviors: lashing out, intense irritability, or becoming overly controlling.

    - Underlying emotion: Fear, masked by a need to regain power.

2. Flight

    - Escaping or avoiding perceived danger by withdrawing or physically leaving.

    - Example behaviors: avoiding certain places or people, overworking, or overplanning. Underlying emotion: Fear, driving a need to feel safe by distancing oneself.

3. Freeze

    - Feeling paralyzed, stuck, or unable to act in the face of danger.

- Example behaviors: dissociation, shutting down emotionally, or "spacing out."

- Underlying emotion: Overwhelming, leading to a shutdown to protect oneself from further harm.

4. Fawn

- Responding to danger by appeasing or accommodating others to avoid conflict or further harm.

- Example behaviors: over-apologizing, people-pleasing, or neglecting one's own needs.

- Underlying emotion: Fear of rejection, abandonment, or harm.

In the chart below, identify how the fight, flight, freeze, or fawn responses may manifest for you personally. Below are some examples of how I showed up in each category.

Fight	Flight	Freeze	Fawn
Example: Aggressively verbally attacking someone	**Example:** Missing counseling appointments	**Example:** Disconnecting in the middle of conversations	**Example:** Trouble establishing healthy boundaries in any relationship

Chapter 3
My Parents: Did they even love me?

Child survivors of sexual abuse are most likely harmed by someone they know, love, and trust. The perpetrator is often a family member or someone who has close proximity to the family. According to RAINN (Rape, Abuse & Incest National Network), 34% of perpetrators in child sex abuse cases are family members[3]. I survived sexual violence and incest. I have only recently, in the last couple of years, started using the term incest to describe my victimization.

While working as a victim advocate, I recall a former clinical supervisor stating that incest was a dated term and we should be calling it what is: *"rape or sexual assault."* Early in my career, this licensed individual influenced me not to use the term. But they were wrong. Incest is different, and the trauma associated with it has different nuances. And, no, I am not playing the trauma Olympics here. All sexual assault traumas have different nuances associated with them, which should be acknowledged and respected. By recognizing these differences, professionals are better equipped to address the different trauma responses and the long-term effects of the abuse.

As a sibling-on-sibling incest survivor, I will always be connected to my perpetrator. We have the same DNA. I have known him my entire life. After being sexually assaulted, we would sit across from the dinner table from each other, sit next to each other in the van on the way to church, or walk together to the pool or baseball practice. To this day, people will walk up to me and say, "Hey,

---

[3] Rape, Abuse & Incest National Network, Incest (2022).
https://www.rainn.org/articles/incest

how is your brother ___ doing? I haven't seen him in a minute." or *"Hey, ain't you ____ little sister? You look just like him."*

I hated the way I looked for years. I would look in the mirror and see resemblances of my perpetrator. This is something that I have only heard from other incest survivors. I had to grow to love my face and believe that I was beautiful. Family members, even after learning about my abuse, would ask me how he was doing. Like, why the hell would I know? Oh, yeah, he is my brother, right?

For me, there was no escaping the connection to my perpetrator when sibling-on-sibling incest was involved. As a professional working in the field, I now know that even if I had told on him when my abuse first started, he might have received counseling, but we would most likely have still been living under the same roof after reunification. That is assuming he would have been removed from the home. For me, it literally meant not escaping my sibling abuser as a child until I was an adult and working through the process of disconnecting myself from what connected us: family.

Being a survivor of incest at an early age had me questioning who I could trust in this world. It made my relationship with my parents difficult. They created the person who caused me harm. I often questioned whether they knew what was happening and decided to protect their oldest child. It impacted my relationship with my parents on so many levels.

I grew up in a middle-class family where my mother was a nurse, and my father was in law enforcement after a military career. On the surface, we looked like the embodiment of stability and structure. But beneath that façade, there were cracks—ones I couldn't unsee as I got older. My parents separated a couple of years after my mother's cancer diagnosis, and while their marriage ended, the lingering effects of their choices on my life remained, both good and bad.

Their parenting style was old school, entrenched in Christianity and patriarchy. My father's authority was absolute. His words were often treated as law in our household. My mother upheld the same structure. To them, questioning their gender-normative views and challenging the inequities was not just rebellious—it was disrespectful.

Even as a young girl, I felt the weight of the inequities placed upon me simply because I was a girl and their only daughter. Why was it my job to clear the table while my brothers got to play? Why was I the one constantly told to "*act like a lady*" while my brothers ran free without care? The feminist in me began to bloom early, and with it came a fire that refused to let me sit silently in the face of unfairness, but at the same time, I remained utterly silent about my abuse.

I pushed back. I challenged their rules. I questioned their authority. I demanded to know *why*. Of course, this didn't go over well. Back then, children did not need to be concerned with why, just do as I say. I was labeled "disrespectful" and "hard-headed." It seemed like I was not just a difficult child—I was *a* difficult child.

But the truth is, I was not intentionally trying to be disrespectful. My resistance was a survival instinct. In a world where my voice had already been silenced by trauma, I was trying to gain some control. Their rigid expectations and inability to see the little girl behind the rebellion only fueled my determination to carve out my own space in a house that seemed stacked against me.

Growing up under these conditions, I often felt alone. My feminism wasn't born out of books or movements. It was born out of necessity. It was my way of fighting back against a world that felt unfair, a household that felt constraining, and a life that felt unchangeable.

Bennie Teresa Stafford, My Mother

As a mother of daughters now, I've gained a new understanding of some of the choices my mother made while raising me. What I once perceived as harshness or even indifference was, in reality, her attempt to protect me, an effort rooted in her own unresolved trauma and the trauma she was experiencing due to being terminally ill. She parented me, her only daughter while carrying the weight of her own pain, a pain I did not fully comprehend until adulthood.

It wasn't until after the family learned about my abuse that a cousin revealed a part of my mother's story: she had been drugged and assaulted while in Chicago during her nursing school years. This revelation, along with other hardships she endured, began to piece together the puzzle of her parenting skills. She had been trying to shield me from the world's harsh realities, unaware that the harm I needed protection from wasn't out there but within our home.

This disconnect—her desire to protect me and her inability to see the abuse I was enduring—laid the groundwork for resentment in our relationship. I thought my mother hated me because I could not feel or recognize her love, even when she was showing it. I do not remember her or my father ever saying, *"I love you."* Not once. Those words were absent from my childhood, and their absence created a void I tried to fill in other ways.

When boys and later men told me they loved me, I believed them, often too quickly, because I was desperate to hear those words. My parents' silence on this front left me searching for affirmation elsewhere. And for years, I was angry with her, not just for not saying she loved me, but for being sick. I irrationally blamed her for having cancer, as if she had any control over her illness. If she weren't sick, I thought *she would have seen what was happening in her house. If she were not sick, I could have told her.*

How could a mother not know? That question haunted me for years and fueled a sense of blame I unfairly placed on her. I now know it was not fair, but at the time, it felt like the only explanation for the pain I carried.

My mother, weighed down by her illness and her own trauma, simply did not have the tools or energy to see what I needed. I wish we had been able to build a relationship outside of the shadow of our traumas, but her death and my inability to communicate my needs prevented that from happening.

While working on sexual assault cases, I saw this dynamic play out repeatedly between mothers and their daughters—resentment rooted in misunderstandings, lack of communication, and pain that neither side had the tools to address. My lived experience allowed me to guide other survivors and their families, helping them understand that these feelings were normal but not insurmountable.

In hindsight, I realize my mother's way of telling me she loved me wasn't through words but actions. Whenever she could, she reminded me she wanted more for me, that she wanted me to have a better life. She kept my siblings and me involved in sports and the arts, and she attended every game or recital she could manage, even when her body was weak. She cared for the elderly in our family and the sick in our church. She was the neighborhood mom, always giving of herself. Her love language was acts of service and quality time—ironically, the same love languages I've come to adopt as an adult. She showed her love, but I could not see it then in the midst of living in my own trauma.

Our relationship was further strained by her discipline style, rooted in old-school parenting and biblical teachings like *"Spare the rod, spoil the child."* For my mother, discipline included physical punishment, and I bore the brunt of it. My brother Benny often reminds me how much I was punished. It was not every day, but it felt like it—whooping's with belts, extension cords, and even slaps across the face.

I rarely saw her or my father discipline my brothers in the same way, which deepened my feelings of isolation and resentment. This dynamic taught me that love and harm could coexist, a lesson that distorted my understanding of relationships.

I began to believe that if someone loved me, they might also hurt me. It was a toxic belief that shaped my self-worth and self-esteem, allowing me to minimize and excuse abusive behavior in later relationships.

Her punishment, layered on top of the abuse I was enduring, made me question the value of my body and my place in the world. My mother's way of loving and disciplining me unintentionally reinforced the belief that my body wasn't my own and that it could be used, punished, or harmed without consequence.

Seeing Her Through a New Lens

As an adult, I now see my mother more clearly—not just as my parent but as a woman navigating her own unhealed wounds. She was not equipped to handle my behavior, my trauma, or even her own. She did the best she could with what she had, and while her methods often hurt me, they were rooted in a desire to save me from the world's ugliness.

Her desire to prepare me for womanhood before she passed added an urgency to her parenting that often felt suffocating. She was trying to teach me everything I needed to know in life as a young lady. These lessons were a lot for me, beginning around the age of twelve. This dynamic, combined with my abuse and her illness, created a relationship filled with tension and missed opportunities for connection.

Looking back, I know she loved me, even if she couldn't say the words. Through her actions—her presence at games, her care for others, her determination to prepare me for life—she showed it. I now wish I could tell her that I see her love, that I understand her choices, and that I forgive her. Her parenting and my experiences shaped me for better and worse. But as I mother my own daughters, I carry forward the lessons I've learned—the ones she taught me and the ones I had to teach myself.

My mother was a devout Christian who attended church often throughout the week, which meant we stayed in church growing up. My mother was a praying woman.

Through her sickness, she never wavered; at least, I never saw her waver in her faith. She would quote the bible and often talk about how my actions were not of God. My relationship with the Church and God is complicated. Being told that I was ungodly while experiencing sexual abuse further deepened the shame and self-blame that I was feeling.

The Church often talked about forgiveness, and so did my mother: *"Forgive others as God forgave you."* I have struggled with that phrase my entire life. Forgive my rapists?? How and why? What would that even look like? Would my mother have wanted me to forgive if I had disclosed what was happening to me? I just couldn't.

Don't get me wrong; my mother was a phenomenal woman. After my parents separated, she did the best she could while battling a terminal illness, depression, and her badass kids. She was a nurse specializing in patients with special needs and geriatrics. She took care of people.

I used to think she cared more about others than she did about me. That was until I had my first daughter at 16 years old. She stopped working as a nurse and opened an in-home daycare. She took care of my daughter to ensure that I graduated from school and even offered to care for her while I went away to college.

Remember, I believe her love language was acts of service and this was how she was showing me love. I decided not to go to college even though I had an opportunity to play collegiate basketball. My daughter was my responsibility and not hers. Plus, I wanted to show her that I was capable of being a great mom. Her love for me and my daughter made it easy for me to maneuver through life as a teenage mom in the beginning.

I wish my mother were alive today, we didn't get a chance to develop a relationship beyond my childhood. I didn't get a chance to show her that I could be more than what I was showing her and the world. My greatest pain is causing her so much pain while she was battling cancer and dealing with my father.

Being sexually abused definitely was the catalyst that impacted our relationship. She deserved better. I deserved better. We deserved better. Because of her, I am very intentional with how I love my daughters, how I feed into their self-worth, and how I show up for them.

Bruce Henry Stafford, Sr., My Father

My father and my abuser had the same name. They had very similar characteristics: dominant, controlling, and misogynistic ideology. The day my brother Quentin disclosed to the family highlighted for me even more that my father was not my protector. When my ex-husband told my father about my abuse, my father never mentioned it to me. My father never checked to see if I was okay, never told me he believed me and never said he was sorry that I had to experience everything I did. I got nothing from him. I felt as though he went on as though he had never been told that his son sexually abused his daughter. As a parent, I'm baffled how this could be his reality.

Yet, when Quentin disclosed his abuse years later, my father's reaction was starkly different. He threatened our abuser's life, giving him a deadline to leave Cleveland or face deadly consequences. There wasn't one person in the family who didn't believe that he would. He was a retired Marine and a master sniper. He would have hunted him down for Quentin. What did my father learn on this particular day that made him want to defend Quentin in the manner he was? What was so different on this day from the day he learned about my abuse? Why wasn't I worthy of the same response years earlier? My father's failure to acknowledge the abuse reinforced a sense of betrayal. I had selfishly expected he would have tried to protect and support me, even retroactively. When this didn't happen, our relationship was never the same.

Family members who knew what was going on were panicking that my father would act upon his threats. I wasn't panicking. Part of me wished he would. I wanted my brother to suffer. I wanted him to hurt. Like I was hurting all of these years later. I was in complete fight mode. My trauma was at the forefront since Quentin's disclosure, along with my father's rejection. In a matter of hours, I experienced back-to-back triggers that left me feeling completely unsafe and vulnerable. And I wasn't my best.

My Aunt Bonnie, who I always thought was someone who would always support me, allowed my rapist to move to Chicago with his daughter and her mom one week later into her empty condo. Her protecting my abuser changed our relationship forever. Our relationship became another that I grieved due to my abuse. It seemed like my abuser had a way of impacting meaningful familial relationships. This is why incest must be addressed holistically and with an understanding of the long-term impact.

Now, I am not sure why my father's response shocked me. Historically, he has failed me. When my parents separated, he moved into a one-bedroom apartment in Euclid, Ohio. My father had the financial ability to afford more than a one-bedroom apartment when he had four kids. We never visited him at his apartment. I stepped foot in his apartment for the first time when my mother kicked me out of the house in the 9th grade and told my father to come to get me. He had been living in his apartment for a couple of years.

I remember sleeping on this hard leather couch in the living room, which became my new bedroom for a week. My father was a Deputy Sheriff with the ranking of a Lieutenant and was the Warden of the County Correction Center. One week after I moved in with him, I was arrested. I remember him coming to one court hearing, and after that, he never visited me again. I didn't see or speak to him the entire time while I was away serving my sentence. I used to make excuses for him about why he wasn't there. Maybe his career prevented him from visiting. Maybe he was just too embarrassed. Years later, while looking through some old family photo albums, I encountered a picture of my family visiting my brother Benny when he was locked up as a juvenile. The picture reminded me of the family trips to support Benny, which included my father. I didn't have any family trips, but my mom, through her sickness, found a way to visit.

When my father found out I was pregnant, he looked me in my face and told me I would never amount to shit and that I had just ruined my life. Those words ran through my veins like blood. They have impacted me in ways that I didn't comprehend until unpacking my relationship with my father during counseling sessions. People always comment on my work ethic and my resiliency. I'm often uplifted for exceeding my professional goals.

Well, folks, it's not just that I have a strong work ethic. My trauma response to my father was proving him wrong, and having my daughter, Aziah, didn't ruin my life. In fact, she saved my life. I vowed that both of us would be more than *just the shit*! I have been working my entire professional career to prove him wrong and make sure that he knew he was wrong. I operated in this manner to the detriment of my mental health. I experienced several rounds of burnout trying to prove him wrong.

After that day when he so eloquently told me that I ruined my life, I didn't see him again until after I had Aziah. He came to the hospital, dropped a couple of cases of baby formula, and left—gifts are my father's love language. I've never been too fond of receiving gifts for the hidden meaning behind them or acting as a substitution for an apology after being wronged, especially when said behavior doesn't change.

Despite spending time in juvenile and being a teen mom, I graduated high school with my graduating class. I received a limited number of graduation tickets and saved one for my father, who said he was coming. My mother, Aunt Bonnie, Aziah, and I waited for him to get to my mother's house as we all planned on going together. It was getting close for us to leave, and he pulled up, stating he couldn't go, and handed me a check. I didn't even look at the check; I just tore it up and walked away. My father couldn't buy away my disappointment or hurt this time.

After high school, I worked several jobs to take care of Aziah while living with her father. I became a state-tested nursing assistant with the thought of going to nursing school in the future. I was fired from the job due to severe understaffing and not appropriately keeping up with my patients. After being fired, I stopped at my mother's house, venting that I needed a job. I had prided myself in working and not relying on the system for assistance. My mother called my father and told him to help get me a job with the county. I initially refused his aid, and my mother, with her wisdom, politely told me not to be a fool.

Several weeks later, I started as the administrative assistant to the Sheriff of our county. After working directly with the Sheriff for a year, he called me into his office to inform me that, starting Monday, I was transferred to the Trips and Transportation Department for county inmates. My heart started racing fast. In my current role, I didn't run into my father often at work. With this transfer, I would now work directly underneath his office. I would now see my father five days out of the week. I hadn't seen that man that much since I was eleven years old.

Working with my father, I saw his sexist and womanizing behavior up close as a young professional female. I met the woman that he had cheated on my mother with throughout their marriage. I would watch him talk down to my co-worker, with whom we shared an office, because of her size. I had my reasons for not liking my father but working with him, I came to realize that I didn't like him as a human. Upon turning twenty-one, I wanted to become a Deputy Sheriff. I spoke with the Sheriff about my intentions, and he informed me that he had to respect my father's wishes. My father had blocked my ability to become a Deputy Sheriff even in his retirement. I could not become a deputy, but I could become a correctional officer. My father had a level of power that I truly did not understand until I matured in my professional career. You might be thinking, how can that happen with a juvenile criminal record? My charges as a juvenile didn't impact my ability to obtain either one of these positions. Working at the Sheriff's Department sparked my interest in the criminal justice system. I went on to become a correctional officer for thirteen years and was one of the first females to join the Special Response Team.

My mother hosted my father's retirement party. She had a way of doing for others when they did not deserve it. During the dinner, my father gave a speech, and instead of thanking my mother, he thanked this lady with whom I secretly knew he was romantically involved in a relationship. I will never forget the look on my mother's face. She was humiliated in front of family, friends, and colleagues. I felt like the 13-year-old kid again who would explode at any given moment. My father and his friend he worked with were walking out the door to the car as though they were escorting my father's *companion* to safety. Once we were outside, I verbally and physically attacked them both. My trauma response to my father often included fight or flight. I decided that day in the winter of 1994 that I was done with my father.

The next time I saw him was at the hospital on July 5, 1995. My mother was rushed to the hospital on July 4th. Her cancer had resurfaced with a force that she never experienced during her years of remission. She underwent emergency surgery. All of my immediate family was there, and my Aunt Bonnie was on her way from Chicago. We were told that the cancer had spread to her pancreas and there wasn't any more they could do for her but keep her comfortable. We stayed at the hospital around the clock. I lashed out at my father, blaming him. My mother was doing well, but her overall health took a turn after the retirement party. I know my father wasn't to blame for her having cancer, but the incident at the retirement party took so much from my mother, and she never really bounced back. My mother died on July 8, 1995.

My Mother's Death

From the time I left home and up until my mother's death, I only engaged with my oldest brother when necessary. My abuse was still pretty much a secret to everyone except for my daughter's father and a counselor who I saw on and off over the years. However, after my mother died, I found myself hanging out a lot with my oldest two brothers. My brother Benny would ask me to come out and to continue my secrecy. My mother's death pushed my siblings and me together. It gave me a sense of normalcy with my siblings outside of my trauma. Yes, my brother caused me harm, but we both just lost our mother, and for some reason, that superseded everything. I was hoping that my mother's death would allow us to move past my abuse. At this time, I craved my brother's love and protection. An outsider might not understand. To be honest, it took me a while to understand why. It was like if I had his love and protection then just maybe he could right his wrongs. Again, this is why, as a professional working in the field and as a survivor, we must acknowledge the nuances that exist within surviving incestuous abuse.

The evening of my mother's funeral, my family was at my mother's house. My father asked for all the siblings to go to the basement to talk. He told me that my mother would want me to move back into the house and raise my daughter. At this time, Quentin moved in with my father and finished high school. Benny was sort of living at home and between one of his girlfriends' houses. My oldest brother wasn't living at home. So, I broke my lease and moved back home. I could afford the mortgage and the bills. Ironically, when I moved back, so did everyone else. Going out with my abuser and my other brother was one thing, but living together was something that I was not mentally prepared for at all.

I was living under the same roof as my abuser again at 18- years-old with my daughter. I was not eating or sleeping. My anxiety was at an all-time high. Living back in my childhood home was a nightmare. The house was filled with memories that I would rather forget. But instead, it was like a movie constantly playing in my head that I could not stop. He never touched me again, but he would intentionally do things that were triggering. When I returned home, my daughter and I slept in my mother's bedroom. I refused to sleep in my old bedroom and did not allow her to sleep without me in the same room. I was like a helicopter mom. Aziah was not allowed to be without me in any part of the house if he was home. The stress of trying to protect her wore me out mentally. I worked overtime to ensure that he was never alone with her. My mother's bedroom was right over his room. He would have these loud sex escapades throughout the night with different women. I would mention to him that I could hear him, and so could his niece. He would just give me this evil smirk. I swear he was the devil. You might be judging me as you read this. But remember, he was not living there when I moved in.

He no longer was sexually abusing me, but the mental abuse and gaslighting were just as damaging. I kept the child support checks from my daughter's father in a fireproof safe under my bed. Someone broke into the safe and stole my checks. Yes, I should have been using a bank, but my immature way of thinking was that if I did not cash them, I wouldn't spend the money. I may have seemed mature to others, but I constantly made very childlike decisions that were not well thought out, like not depositing my child support checks. I still have this safe today with the damaged key lock. Strange things kept happening while living back at home. One evening, while coming home from being with some friends, my daughter and I entered the house to find a burglary in progress. I grabbed my daughter and ran out of the house. The burglars were in the basement, rummaging through the area of the house where my oldest brother resided. He was a known drug dealer, and I later learned that he was pimping out females. So not only was he a rapist, but he also trafficked women for financial gain. How could I be a fool and think that moving back to this dysfunctional, trauma-filled house with my daughter was the right decision?

Suicidal thoughts crept into my mind consistently. I was severely depressed and was struggling with life. Driving to work in the morning, I often thought about driving off the 480 bridge or would find myself daydreaming of ending my life.

Masking was something that I perfected. No one knew I was feeling this way. My oldest daughter is the reason why I am alive. If I killed myself, who would take care of her? Would my rapist now have access to her? I felt so alone in a world with so many people. I swallowed my pride and asked my father for help. I wanted him to tell his sons to leave the house. They were not contributing financially, and my daughter and I weren't safe. I just knew he would help because of his granddaughter, but silly me, he didn't, and I had to make some hard decisions. I met this older guy who had moved back home from the military. We were dating, but nothing too serious. We took a quick trip to Virginia Beach so he could sign his divorce papers.

My daughter stayed with my godparents. When I returned, the majority of my items in the house were gone. My brothers thought I had just left and was not coming back. Well, at least this is what I later learned they were telling family members. Things got really scary for me at the house. My daughter and I ended up moving in with my now ex-husband after only knowing him for several months. See, desperate people do desperate things. I was making one decision after another just to survive.

My ex-husband eventually bridged the gap between my father and me. They formed a relationship, and he became a pretty good grandfather to my daughters. As he got older, his health declined due to a car accident that damaged his back. He was staying in a bungalow. The tenant in my rental had to leave, and my father needed a ranch-style house. Allowing him to rent my property benefited us both. He needed the space, and I needed someone who could pay the rent that I could trust to pay the rent. My father did a lot of things, but financially, he took care of his business. As I think back, it is so ironic that the child that he told would not be shit is now his landlord!

My marriage was struggling for several reasons, and I did not think it would last much longer. I started looking for an apartment to move into with my youngest daughter, Taylor. I was so stressed out trying to find an apartment, work, and deal with the pending separation that I came up with the idea to move into my rental property with my father temporarily. I seem to have a pattern of coming up with ideas that will only further complicate things and cause me harm in the future. This is me surviving. It always seemed like I was finding ways to survive. Survival became a goal for every day. For some reason living on my own scared me, and I wanted my daughters to have a similar living arrangement that they had when I was married. I had a whole house, but my father was living there. After having a conversation with my father, I moved in. It was like he was happy to have me there. Maybe it was his way of making up for the previous years. Just perhaps, I could finally have a parental relationship that the little girl inside of me has longed for.

Why the f%$k do I keep setting myself up for failure in this area? Kids naturally seek parental approval, and those who experience trauma often seek parental validation through adulthood. I did not truly understand the impact of living with my father until later when we were no longer living together again. I found myself angry, depressed, consistently on the defense, and regularly operating in flight and fight response. I went back to my counselor to address my feelings towards my father. I really did not like this man. Growing up in church, I learned the Ten Commandments and was taught they are the tenets that Christians should follow. The Fifth Commandment: "*Honor your father and your mother, as the Lord your God commanded you, that your days may be long, and that it may go well with you in the land that the Lord your God is giving you.*" In honoring my father, I caused harm to myself mentally. I struggled so much with my faith because of my trauma.

My father was older and had a lot of medical issues. He needed someone to help him, and I was the sibling in the position to assist since he lived with me. But his living with me was not helpful to my mental health. I had finally gotten to a point where I was starting to thrive in every area— except when it came to dealing with my father.

Counseling helped me to see that honoring my father did not have to be to the detriment of my mental health. I can honor from a distance. I can honor from a place that centers my mental well-being. With his healthcare needs changing and the realization that I did not have to lose myself caring for him, I moved him into an assisted living facility. I felt a sense of freedom that was equivalent to when I was locked up as a juvenile and free from my brother's abuse. Freedom is not always pretty.

Taking care of him over the next couple of years was very triggering for me. He needed me and there were times it was a struggle to be there for him when he lacked consistency in being there for me. The impact of child sexual abuse was still impacting me thirty years later. There were days that I had to ask my daughters to step up and take the lead. I chose to protect myself. Others looking in might judge me for how I handled things. Hell, before counseling I might have been one of those people judging others. Counseling helped me to be comfortable centering myself and my mental health in decisions that will impact me. Stepping back from the day-to-day with my father was best for both of us. I know that I couldn't give him my best and even he deserved better. My way of honoring him was recognizing my limitations and allowing others to assist him.

A couple of years after placing him in the assisted living facility, he died at the age of 87 while I was vacationing in the Dominican Republic. I recall going into the steam room at the spa after having my traditional vacation massage and crying. I cried secretly for what seemed like forever, but realistically, it was more like a few minutes. The day in the living room when I exploded upon learning that my father knew about my abuse but stayed silent, I knew I had to stop expecting something from my father that he was just simply incapable of giving. His death finalized this reality. I was crying because I would never experience the love and protection from my father that I desired. I no longer had a parent on this earth. Something about this realization sparked a desire to love my daughters even more and build a legacy of love and support that will carry them through.

During my healing journey, I've come to recognize how deeply grief from the loss of relationships—whether due to death or the repositioning of someone in my life—has shaped me in ways I didn't always understand. Today, I have a clearer awareness of what my grief looks and feels like. I have learned to lean into vulnerability, giving myself permission to build meaningful connections, even knowing that grief may one day accompany them. Allowing myself to feel deeply and trust again has been a crucial step in my healing process—a step toward reclaiming my ability to love, connect, and grow.

Chapter Activities: Embracing Grief and Rebuilding Trust in Relationships

Objective: To reflect on the impact of grief from lost or repositioned relationships and to foster self-awareness, vulnerability, and trust in building meaningful connections as part of your healing journey.

Part 1: Identifying Grief in Your Life

Take a moment to reflect on how grief has shown up in your life. Use the following prompts to guide your journaling:

1. **Recognizing Loss:**

   - Write about a relationship you have lost, whether through death, distance, change, or trauma.

   - How has this loss impacted you emotionally, mentally, or physically?

2. **Understanding Your Grief:**

   - What does grief look like for you? (e.g., sadness, anger, isolation, physical exhaustion, etc.)

   - How do you typically respond when you feel grief? (e.g., withdrawing, seeking comfort, avoiding emotions, etc.)

3. **Lessons from Loss:**

   - What have you learned about yourself through this loss?

   - Has it shaped how you approach new relationships? If so, how?

Part 2: Exploring Vulnerability

Instructions:
Write about your relationship with vulnerability and trust:

1. **Trusting Again:**

    - What fears come up when you think about opening yourself to new relationships?

    - What would it take for you to feel safe trusting someone again?

2. **Reframing Vulnerability:**

    - Reflect on a time when being vulnerable led to a positive outcome. What made that experience feel safe?

    - Write an affirmation about vulnerability, such as, *"I am strong enough to embrace vulnerability as part of my growth."*

Part 3: Actionable Trust-Building

Objective: To take intentional steps toward nurturing trust in new or existing relationships.

1. **Create a Trust Inventory:**

    - List three people in your life you feel you can trust or would like to build trust with.

    - Next to each name, write one small action you can take to deepen your connection (e.g., share a feeling, ask for support, express appreciation).

2. **Set a Goal:**

- Commit to taking one of these actions this week and journal about how it felt to practice trust and vulnerability.

Chapter 4
Intimate Relationships:
Seeking Control, Protection and Love

The school year at MLK ended quietly, without any more incidents, and for a brief moment, I felt at peace. But that summer, everything shifted. My brother came home from college with no plans to return in the fall. The fragile sense of safety I'd found in his absence vanished as quickly as I did whenever he came near. To escape, I began seeking solace in relationships—different guys, often much older than me.

Fighting became a thing of the past; instead, I found myself in relationships with much older men. For the first time, I felt like I was in control of my body, like I had some say over who I was and what I did. It was a kind of freedom—one that felt powerful, even if only for a moment. Sometimes, I left home for days, seeking spaces where I could breathe freely, where I could feel that fake semblance of control.

My mother would come looking for me. She would always bring me home if she found me, calling me fast, ungodly, and praying all the way back home in between yelling at me. She would ask God to change my behavior. I would sit there quietly, wondering where God was when I was being abused. I am not sure which one of my friends or brothers would snitch me out, but she almost always found me. Mind you, this was before social media and cell phones. As I look back on it, my mother showed her love by always looking for me. She never gave up on me. She knew I could be greater than what I was presenting but struggled with how to support me through the process beyond praying for me.

I finished high school at John Marshall on the west side of Cleveland, where the majority of the students were from Whitney

Young Junior High School. Reconnecting with old faces and making new friends came easily. People didn't bother me. I had the reputation of being a fighter, and honestly, at this point, I was tired of fighting. I was a different person. Things seemed to be looking up—I was attending school, playing sports, and, most importantly, I was not being abused. For the first time in a long while, life felt manageable.

Then I met him. He was older, charismatic, and attentive in ways that seemed perfect to my trauma-brained self. He bought me things, took me on dates, and, most importantly, he listened to me. For hours, we shared our trauma stories—his childhood marked by an abusive, alcoholic father, mine by incest, and the constant battle for survival. It felt deep, intimate, and real.

But what I didn't know then was that we weren't connecting in a healthy way. We were bonding because of our trauma, entangling ourselves in a relationship where our pain became the glue. I depended on him for everything: protection, love, and even my happiness. This dependence gave him power over me, power no one should have over another person.

He was the first person that I told about my brother harming me. He shared with me that his father was an alcoholic and would beat his mother him, and his siblings. We connected through our trauma. I depended on him so much. No, I depended on him for too much. I sought him out to make me happy. I now know that no one should have that much control over another person's emotions. The honeymoon phase of our relationship didn't last long. His true representative showed up and mirrored his father, an alcoholic who was abusive.

Bonding through trauma at this time in my life was unhealthy and dangerous. It was dangerous in this situation as we both hadn't taken the necessary steps to start healing from our trauma. We became co-dependent on each other. Bonding through trauma can be unhealthy when it develops into emotional codependency, re-enforces negative behavior, and fosters toxic dynamics and power imbalances. All of these were present in this relationship.

I found myself pregnant at 16 years old. He wanted me to have an abortion, but my mother did not believe in abortions. Since I was underage, I would need her signature to have an abortion, which was not happening due to her religious beliefs. Truth be told, I did not know if I even wanted to have an abortion, but with the abuse I was now experiencing, having an abortion seemed logical. I found out that I could petition the court to give me permission to have an abortion without parental consent. Since I was already familiar with the court house, this task did not seem too scary.

In 1992, the most common way for a minor to obtain an abortion without the consent of her parent, guardian, or custodian was for the minor to get a juvenile court order stating that she was sufficiently mature and properly informed to make the decision or that obtaining the consent was not in her best interests. Please note the law requiring parental consent changed during the early 2000's.

I went through the court process and it was determined that I could have the abortion without parental consent. I attended these hearings by myself. My child's father was afraid to attend because he was several years older than me and we didn't know if he would get in trouble.

I was so confused as to what I truly wanted to do. I wanted to keep my baby, but I was afraid. I was afraid of not being a good mother. I was afraid my child would experience the horrors of the world that I did. I was afraid that my child would witness their mother being beaten by an alcoholic just like their father witnessed while growing up. I was afraid that I wouldn't be able to protect my child.

But I wanted my child. I wanted to love my child and have someone love me back unconditionally, and I didn't want to further disappoint my mother.

Several days later, I lied and told him they denied me the right to have an abortion without parental consent. I thought lying was safer than telling the truth, that I wanted to keep my baby. A decision that was my right. It was also my right if I wanted to go through with the abortion as well. However, lying in the moment was survival, or so I thought it was. He wasn't happy about this. I remember vividly the day he punched me in my stomach and attacked me, hoping that I lost the baby. I should have ended things with him that day, but by this time in my life, I've become accustomed to people inflicting violence upon me.

I gave birth to a beautiful baby girl named Aziah Charae on September 19, 1992. We were basically living with him before I graduated high school. I left one house full of dysfunction and trauma only to move into another one. There were signs at the beginning that I completely ignored, or because of my trauma, I didn't think what I was experiencing early in the relationship was that bad. I saw a post on Facebook recently that stated, *"Unhealed trauma can cause you to downplay mistreatment because you've survived worse."* I lived in this space mentally for many years.

What I originally saw as him being protective was actually him being overbearing and controlling. He gave me my first car but would later take the license plates, so I couldn't drive. He wanted to know my every move and quickly started isolating me from my friends and family. In my immaturity, I accepted this as love and him wanting us to spend all our time together. To this day, I contemplate whether it was the physical violence or verbal abuse that was worse. He was constantly demeaning me and telling me nobody else would want me because I was damaged goods. My daughter's father took my trauma and hurled it at me whenever he didn't get his way or when he was intoxicated.

The drinking was the catalyst for him becoming physically violent. He saw his father behave in this manner. He normalized his behavior. In my mind, because I fought back, I wasn't in an abusive relationship. I wasn't experiencing domestic violence. This term wasn't something that I was overly familiar with. I was in denial and making up all types of excuses to condone his behavior—because, yet again, in my mind, I was allowing yet another person to cause me harm.

Living in denial was easier than acknowledging at 17 years old that I was a victim of incest, rape, and now domestic violence. According to the Ohio Domestic Violence Network (2022)[4], 1 in 5 teens who have been in a serious relationship report being hit, slapped, or pushed by a partner. Another alarming statistic is that adolescent girls in physically abusive relationships were 3.5 times more likely to become pregnant than non-abused girls. I strongly believe that I was in this abusive relationship as a direct result of the sexual abuse I experienced at a young age.

Drinking brought out the worst in my daughter's father—he was an angry, aggressive, and obnoxious drunk. Our daughter, Aziah, was a toddler and I didn't want her to grow up witnessing her parents fighting and her father's drunken episodes. I tried to reason with him to stop drinking and to seek help. What the heck was I thinking? I tried to have this conversation numerous times and to no avail, nothing changed. One afternoon of drinking and arguing our downstairs neighbors complained about the noise. Their complaints incited him and the police were called.

---

[4] Ohio Domestic Violence Network (2022). https://www.odvn.org/children-teens-and-parents/children-and-teens/

When the police arrived, I didn't intervene or try to stop them. I wanted to yell, take his ass to jail, and keep him there! I saw his arrest as an opportunity to leave the relationship quietly. At least, that is what I thought. While he was in jail, I moved in with a friend and her kids. When an individual decides to leave an abusive relationship, it can become the most dangerous time in the relationship. Upon making bail he came home to an empty house. I left and vowed to myself and my daughter that I would never go back.

When I go to restaurants and other public places, I always sit facing the door. I do this partially because of my thirteen years working as a correctional officer. At least, this is what I have always told myself and others. The reality is after leaving my daughter's father, he stalked me for several months. He was following me to and from work, popping up to places where I was hanging out with friends, and sitting outside my house watching me.

I was working for the Sheriff during this time as his administrative assistant. I was too embarrassed to let anyone know what was going on. If I did, my father would most certainly find out. I could hear his words echoing in my head when he said to me that I wouldn't amount to shit when he found out I was pregnant. And here I am, leaving an abusive relationship and now being stalked. I felt like shit. Maybe he was right about me! Being stalked added a level of anxiety and hypervigilance I had never experienced through my trauma. I never knew when he would surface and what state of mind he would be in if he did.

One night, I went out with my roommate. Her cousin spent the night at our house watching the kids. We both were single mothers who worked and took care of our responsibilities. A night out without the kids was a treat and well-deserved.

After being out for a couple of hours, we received a 911 page. I didn't have a cell phone yet—I was still rocking my pager. We left the club and rushed home to find the police at our house. My daughter's father had broken into our house and wanted to know where I was. The babysitter was able to call the police and he ran through the backyard of the house once he heard the police sirens. He was eventually arrested and charged with two different cases of attempted burglary.

Now, remember, I'm the Sheriff's assistant at this time and now I have to meet with an assistant county prosecutor at the Justice Center, which is the same building where I work. All of this was just too embarrassing. I met with a county prosecutor and informed them I didn't want him to go to trial. I just wanted him to leave me alone, seek treatment, and support his child. I don't know if I was making this decision out of fear or feeling sorry for him and not wanting him to go to prison. Like the majority of criminal cases, he pled to lesser charges of attempted aggravated burglary. He was sentenced to probation and drug treatment and required to pay child support.

I extended grace to him because I understood his trauma. But, grace was not extended to him with our daughter. After several attempts at trying to maintain my daughter's relationship with her father, his drinking and toxic behavior required me to protect my daughter and prevent him from seeing her until he changed his life. She would not be harmed due to the lack of me providing her protection as a mother. After a long period of him not paying child support, he was arrested and I had to appear in court. I went to court, and I informed them that I didn't want child support. I wanted nothing from him and walked away.

After this relationship ended, I went back to what was comfortable for me, seeking comfort in the wrong places. This was around the time after my mother's death that I started engaging with counselors for the first time seriously. I knew that even though I wasn't exposing my daughter to my shenanigans, she was indirectly impacted—and I wanted more for her, more for us. It was time to start doing the work and focusing on my mental health. I wanted to be a good mom, a good human. I wanted my daughter to have a family that would love her. So, my next relationship would focus on finding her a father figure and some stability. And the main guy that I was seeing at this time wasn't the one.

I met my ex-husband shortly after my mother died in the summer of 1995. We clicked immediately and connected through our children. He just returned home from the military and was in the final stages of his second divorce. Within months of meeting, Aziah and I moved in with him. It wasn't planned at all. I was still living in hell at the family house with ALL of my brothers. We took a trip to Virginia Beach and when I came home, many of my items were no longer there. For some reason, it was assumed that I moved and abandoned my things. This was my brother's way of pushing me out. Being away for a couple of days made me realize just how stressful living at home was.

I needed to provide my daughter some stability because, at this point, she had lived in 5 different places and she was only 3 years old. We needed a safe place to stay and he gave us that. My daughter needed a father figure and he provided that. I needed protection and he gave me that. I was again making a decision that would impact our lives on the need to survive. This relationship lasted seventeen years. During this seventeen-year period, I didn't disclose my abusive past until around year fourteen. I am not sure why I kept it a secret for so long. By this time, my marriage was barely surviving due to infidelity, secrets, dysfunctional familial relationships, and a desire on my part to seek personal happiness and growth.

After my divorce, I approached relationships leading with what some might call my masculine energy. For me, this surfaced as I dated multiple men at a time while leading with dominance, independence, goal-orientation, and directness. I often heard that I was not very emotional or expressive with my inner feelings. Now, remember, I am not talking about all women. I am just saying this is how my masculine energy showed up. I was having the time of my life! Traveling, building my career, dating, and moving how I wanted.

I felt in control. But nonetheless, I also knew that how I was moving was counter to my long-term desire to be in a healthy relationship and be married. But dating and not moving right into a relationship gave me a better understanding of who I am, what I desire from a partner, my boundaries, and my ability to live in my truth about my past. My sista-friend, Kelly, called me out on my actions.

Several years after my divorce, I shared that I wanted a real relationship. I wanted to find my person. She told me I needed to clean my closet. Translation: stop your dumb shit. I ignored her advice for a while because, hey, I was having fun. But the fun only fills a short-term desire. I really wanted fun with love, protection, a safe haven, a supportive partner, an accountability partner—I wanted my person. We all have our own desires when it comes to intimate relationships. We just need to be honest with ourselves to ensure we are making decisions from a healthy space and not from our trauma.

I stopped my dating shenanigans and engaged in celibacy for a couple of years. During this time period, I met a couple of folks and went on dates, but nothing materialized. This period of time allowed me to focus on myself and really engage in dating from a different perspective for me, a healthy perspective. I was dating with the intention of being in a healthy, supportive relationship where we each have done the work to address our past traumas. Because at this point, who can say they haven't had any trauma in life that might impact how they show up in an intimate relationship? Setting this boundary limited my dating experience. And many couldn't understand why I remained single for so long. I wasn't going to compromise on what I knew would be foundational for any intimate relationship.

I was no longer willing to sacrifice the hard work I have accomplished through counseling and all those co-pays to settle for someone who might not understand why I maneuver the way I do or someone who hasn't been willing to do the hard work for themselves. In the midst of writing this book, I found my person. The person who understands me or seeks to understand me when they don't. The person who protects me but doesn't demean me. The person who allows me to make mistakes and gives me my space while holding me accountable. The person who makes me laugh and even cry because I knew I deserved this type of love but wasn't sure if it would find me. Ironically, we first met when I returned home from Scioto Village at MLK High School when I was in the 10th grade.

We married in Grenada on October 24, 2024. My relationship with Damon Wright is the first one where I get to choose my partner, not from a place of survival but a place of love and friendship. In doing so, it's the first relationship I've entered completely naked. No, I don't mean naked in the literal sense, but naked where I'm vulnerable—sharing and allowing my femininity to be front and centered.

Trust me, I am still a work in progress in this area. Because of how we both approached the relationship, we are experiencing a different type of love together. Tapping into my femininity has been healing and rewarding and allowed space for him to lead in a healthy manner. It allowed me to not have to carry the weight of the world or my trauma.

Chapter Activities: Reflecting on Intimacy, Control, and Healthy Love

This activity is designed to help you reflect on past and present intimate or platonic relationships, identify patterns of behavior or thought that may stem from trauma, and explore how to build healthier connections moving forward.

Step 1: Exploring Relationship Patterns

Take 10-15 minutes to journal your responses to the following questions:

1. Reflect on your past relationships. What were the main reasons you entered into these relationships? (e.g., love, companionship, safety, validation, fear of being alone, etc).

2. Were there any common behaviors or dynamics in those relationships that you now recognize as unhealthy? (e.g., control, dependence, lack of boundaries, or neglecting your own needs).

3. How did those relationships impact your sense of self-worth or identity?

Step 2: Identifying Red and Green Flags

Using a sheet of paper, create two columns labeled **Red Flags** and **Green Flags**. Reflect on your past and current relationships to complete the columns:

- **Red Flags:** List behaviors or patterns that made you feel unsafe, disrespected, or undervalued. Examples might include controlling behaviors, manipulation, lack of communication, or dismissiveness.

- **Green Flags:** List positive behaviors that made you feel supported, valued, and loved. Examples might include active listening, respect for boundaries, emotional stability, and mutual trust.

Step 3: Understanding Trauma Responses

Answer the following prompts:

1. How has your past trauma influenced the way you approach relationships?

2. Do you recognize any specific trauma responses (e.g., fight, flight, freeze, or fawn) in your relationships? How have they shown up?

3. What are some healthier ways you could address these responses in future or current relationships?

Chapter 5
Parenting Through Trauma:
I can't F&^ this up!*

Parenting is challenging on its own, but parenting while actively dealing with depression and the impact of trauma adds a layer of complexity that's hard to explain to those who haven't experienced it. For years, I walked through life carrying the weight of my childhood trauma without fully understanding the toll it had taken on me emotionally, mentally, and physically. Depression or mental health was another topic that my family did not discuss. It was not that they did not believe in mental health. They never learned about how to truly address it outside prayer and the church.

When people around me commented that I "had no emotions" or always "*seemed irritated,*" I did not know how to respond. The truth was, I was feeling too much, not too little. Depression wrapped itself around me like a fog. Every small frustration felt enormous, and every slight inconvenience felt like another failure. It was not until I was diagnosed with post-traumatic stress disorder (PTSD) and depression that I began to understand what was happening inside me and how to manage it.

For years, I parented my daughters while struggling silently with my mental health. My mental health did not just affect me—it affected them, too. Children are perceptive, and even when we try to shield them from our struggles, I am sure my daughters felt the tension, the heaviness, and the emotional absence.

I can admit now that my depression shaped the way I parented. There were times when I found myself not speaking to my daughters with love, even though I had nothing but love for them. I was not cussing at them or calling them names, but my responses were often short or sprinkled with irritation. To them, it may have felt like I was upset with them when, in reality, I wasn't. I was often overwhelmed and in a state of hypervigilance, particularly when they reached the age when I first experienced trauma.

Depression does not always look the same for everyone, and as a Black woman, it often wore a different mask for me. Put that on top of me already sharing with you all that I mastered the concept of masking at an early age.

Some recent research is shedding light on how depression in Black women may present differently compared to their counterparts, a reality shaped by a combination of cultural, social, and systemic factors. This culturally responsive understanding is long overdue, as many Black women—including myself—have struggled with undiagnosed or misdiagnosed depression, navigating life with symptoms that do not always align with the theoretical textbook definitions.

For me, depression did not show up in its classical manner. Instead, it manifested as emotional exhaustion, which made it difficult for me to connect with others beyond the surface. At times, irritability and anger bubbled to the surface, and in a society quick to label Black women as "angry," those feelings were often dismissed or misinterpreted. I had an increased level of hypervigilance. I felt like I had to be alert all the time because something negative was bound to happen—a direct response to being in survival mode for the majority of my life.

The *superwoman syndrome* is often not associated with depression. This is perhaps one of the most insidious ways depression manifests in Black women. The pressure to be everything to everyone—the strong one, the dependable one, the one who never breaks—was not just external; it became internalized. I felt like I had to keep going, no matter how much I was struggling inside. I was battling my own internal struggles and trying to be a present-loving parent.

Shifting my approach to parenting

A turning point came after my divorce when I sought counseling. This was not the first time I had been in therapy, but this time, the focus shifted to how I parented my daughters and how I could create healthier dynamics in our relationship. My counselor helped me unlock tools I already had but wasn't adequately using.

One of the most transformative lessons I learned was the power of listening—not just hearing my daughters but genuinely *listening* to their needs and understanding how I could support them rather than always trying to fix everything. My instinct to fix came from a place of love, but it often came across as perfectionism. I was projecting my desire for them to have a "perfect" life by swooping in to solve their problems before they had the chance to navigate them on their own. My youngest daughter, Taylor, would eventually tell me she did not need me to fix everything. The last thing I wanted to do was create a dynamic where they relied on me for the simplest things as they navigated young adulthood.

I started giving them the space to be vulnerable, take chances, and make mistakes. This was not easy for me—my trauma had taught me that mistakes could lead to pain and that vulnerability was dangerous. But through counseling, I realized that shielding my daughters from every possible hardship was not protecting them— it was stifling their growth.

Another transformative shift in our relationship came when I chose to share my trauma story with them. Talking openly about my experiences, including my counseling journey and mental health struggles, became a way to build trust and connection. I wanted them to know it is okay to seek help, feel deeply, and ask for support when needed.

By normalizing conversations about mental health, I hoped to break the cycle of silence. I wanted my daughters to know that they did not have to carry their struggles alone. Through these conversations, we are building a foundation of openness and vulnerability that strengthens our bond.

These changes did not happen overnight. It took time, effort, and a willingness to engage in self-reflection. But as I started to shift the way I parented, I saw shifts in my daughters, too. They began to share more with me—about their fears, their dreams, and even their mistakes. They knew they had a safe space to land without judgment or immediate solutions.

Parenting with this new approach did not just help my daughters. It helped me, too. It allowed me to see them as individuals capable of navigating their own journeys, and it reminded me that my role was not to control their path but to walk alongside them while being one of their biggest cheerleaders.

Today, I parent with a greater awareness of how my mental health impacts my children and how my parenting impacts their mental health. I have worked to repair the areas where my struggles may have created cracks. I have learned to speak with love, to listen without the need to fix, and to show up with vulnerability and authenticity.

Trauma and depression may have shaped parts of my parenting journey, but it did not define it. What defines it is the love I have for my daughters and the intentional steps I have taken to ensure they know that love—through my words, my actions, and my presence. My daughters have seen me matriculate through my healing journey and through that, I hope they have learned that it is okay to be imperfect, to be vulnerable, and always to choose themselves.

Beautiful Black Mother

Beautiful Black Mother that you are, you have raised me to be a productive young lady.

With your laid back personality, and motherly love, I thank you for being that beautiful black mother to me.

From the tough love I was given at times to the caring arms you've given me, I will always love you.

Beautiful Black Mother with the long black hair, milk chocolate skin, and loving smile, you have inspired me to go the extra mile.

You are special, a gift from above. Beautiful Black Mother, you are a cherished treasure to love.

You have been with me through thick and thin. Even when times were rough, you still kept that big grin.

Beautiful Black Mother, you're patient when I'm foolish, you can do almost anything, you give guidance when I ask, and you're the master of every task.

Without you, there would be no me. Your love, your attention, and your guidance have made me who I am. You have shown me the way to serve, to accomplish, to persevere.

Because of you, my Beautiful Black mother, I have joy, contentment, satisfaction, and peace.

I love you more than you know. You have my total respect.
If I had a choice of mothers, you'd be the only one I select!

My Beautiful Black mother, nobody's equal to you.
With you in my life, I'm blessed. I love you and want you to know I
think you're the very best.

Written in middle school by Aziah Kado, my oldest daughter

Chapter Activities: Fostering Connection and Healing Through Parenting

Objective: This activity is designed to help you reflect on how your mental health has influenced your parenting, identify areas for growth, and create actionable steps to strengthen your relationship with your children through intentional connection and vulnerability.

Building Bridges Through Listening

Instructions: This activity focuses on active listening and creating space for your children to express themselves.

1. **Set the Stage:**

   - Choose a time to sit down with your child(ren) one-on-one.

   - Create a safe and comfortable environment where they feel encouraged to share.

2. **Practice Active Listening:**

   - Ask open-ended questions like:

     - *What's been on your mind lately?*

     - *Is there anything I can do to support you more?*

     - *How do you feel about the way we communicate?*

   - Focus on listening without interrupting, offering advice, or jumping in to fix the problem (my youngest daughter taught me this).

3. **Affirm Their Feelings:**
   - Use affirming statements to show you value their emotions, such as:

     - *"I hear you, and I understand why you feel that way."*

     - *"Thank you for sharing that with me."*

   - Acknowledge their courage in being vulnerable with you.

4. **Reflect on the Experience:**
   - After the conversation, write about how it felt to listen without trying to fix it.

   - Did you learn anything new about your child? Did this exercise deepen your connection?

Little Teresa around 8 years old!

Bennie Teresa Stafford, my mother

Bruce H. Stafford, Sr., my father

A teen mom at 16 years old

11th grade at John Marshall High School

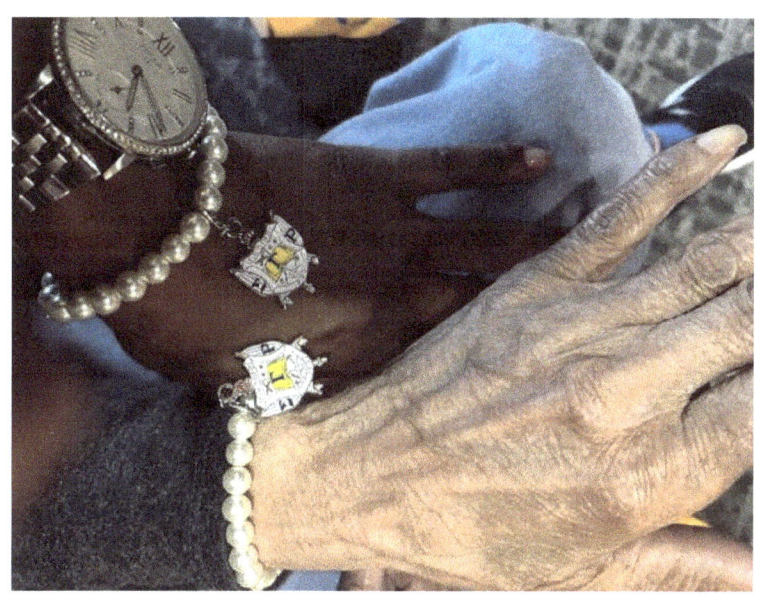

My Aunt Bonnie, My Soror

Getting ready to train!

My loves!

At the Black Women's March in Washington, D.C.

Proud member of Sigma Gamma Rho Sorority, Inc.

#ForeverWright2024

Part 2
Beyond Surviving

Chapter 6
Letting Go: Focusing on What I Can Control

At my lowest points, I did not think I would survive. There were moments when the weight of my experiences felt unbearable, and the thought of ending it all crept into my mind constantly. Over the years, I made several plans to take my life with one attempt. Yet, here I am—not just surviving but thriving. I thank God for saving me and answering my prayers.

When I was locked up at Scioto Village, I learned the Serenity Prayer: *"God grant me the serenity to accept the things I cannot change, courage to change the things I can, and the wisdom to know the difference."*

The Serenity Prayer has stayed with me over the years as a source of inspiration and focus, a guidepost in the moments of darkness and struggle. Although I had this complicated relationship with religion and my trauma, I had to believe in something greater than myself, something unseen, in order for me to believe that my life could be something different. I had to develop faith and fully understand what this meant for me on a spiritual level.

My journey required releasing the version of myself that had been created for survival, a version that protected the little girl inside me but no longer served the woman I wanted to become. I held onto the realization that while I could not control the horrific things that happened to me—the sexual violence, domestic abuse, or the absence of healthy love and protection—I could develop the power over how I responded to my trauma. Obtaining the power to push through my trauma became my focus. This is where my faith kicked in. I had to believe in a version of myself that was not fully developed.

This concept was not easy. It was challenging. It required me to have some uncomfortable conversations with myself, with my therapist, and those that mattered to me the most. I cannot pinpoint exactly when this shift occurred partially because it was a gradual process that even I did not initially recognize. At some point, while married and working in the gender-based violence field, I realized I had a lot more work to complete. I knew there was a better version of me than what I was presenting.

I still had a lot of hatred in my heart. I was hurting. I was still not receiving the protection and love that I deserved. The infidelity in my first marriage sent me back to a scary place in my life.

A time when I did not see the value in myself. I found myself in victim mode, and in this mode, I did not operate at my best. I started secretly seeing a therapist again. It was with her that I took a deeper dive into unpacking my childhood trauma and how it showed up in my life as an adult. It was the first time that I started making the connection between my historical trauma and how it shows up in my present-day reality. I joined a support group with other women and started sharing with them about my abuse. Counseling normalized my reality.

Counseling also gave me an understanding that I could be different and that the constant fear, pain, paranoia, sadness, and all these other emotions that would take over did not have to be at the forefront. Like, I could really control or mitigate how I showed up and responded to situations. This whole time, I was focused more on what had happened to me than on living an abundant life. The *woe-is-me* mentality was real. Asking God if he even loved me. If so, why did he let these things happen to me? I focused so much on the past instead of the present and the future that I am sure I missed opportunities for growth and love.

This shift was the beginning of me acknowledging all that I have experienced and being thankful that I did survive. But I did not want to just survive. I wanted more. Now, don't get me wrong, once I discovered this, it wasn't like I didn't have my setbacks. Remember, healing is not linear, and it isn't pretty either. Healing and addressing one's trauma requires a high level of self-reflection. On the path to wholeness and healing, there were times I had setbacks. These setbacks were lessons that would prepare me for the future and propelled me further.

For instance, night terrors or nightmares are something that would set me back. I felt that since I had unpacked my trauma and met it head-on with my therapist, I should not be having night terrors or nightmares. I am talking about it. I am no longer in denial, so why am I still having these issues? In a session, I was able to connect that I would have them when I did not feel safe, experiencing a lot of stress, and when I did not have trust within my intimate relationships. My marriage was having a lot of trust-related issues, so it made sense that I was having more night terrors or intrusive thoughts about my traumatic experiences.

My therapist eventually diagnosed me with post-traumatic stress disorder (PTSD). A disorder in which a person has difficulty recovering after experiencing or witnessing a terrifying event. PTSD may last months or years, with triggers that can bring back memories of the trauma accompanied by intense emotional and physical reactions. Symptoms may include nightmares or unwanted memories of the trauma, avoidance of situations that bring back memories of the trauma, heightened reactions, anxiety, or depressed mood. Treatment includes different types of trauma-focused psychotherapy as well as medications to manage symptoms.

For the majority of my life, I self-medicated with alcohol, marijuana, and sex to mask the symptoms and feelings associated with them. Working with my counselor, I gained new and healthier tools to assist me with coping with my trauma. This was truly the beginning of developing my toolkit that would move me beyond just surviving. Upon first receiving the diagnosis of PTSD, I was like naw, I do not have that. The diagnosis initially questioned my ability to be a victim advocate. Was I too broken, too damaged, to help people?

How could I truly help others when parts of me still felt so broken? This question weighed heavily on me as I stepped deeper into my work with survivors. I quickly realized that if I were not intentional about addressing my own trauma, I could unintentionally project my experiences onto those I was meant to support. Survivors are incredibly intuitive, and I knew they would sense when I was not fully present for them.

I had to work through the difficult process of separating my pain from theirs. This meant addressing my triggers head-on and ensuring that I was responding to their needs, not overlaying my own. I learned to intentionally slow down during conversations, resisting the urge to "*fix*" or lead them toward decisions I thought were best. Instead, I focused on centering their voices, asking thoughtful questions, and empowering them to determine the path that best suited their unique journey.

By providing survivors with all the information they needed to make informed decisions, I was not only honoring their autonomy but also giving them something I had longed for during my own healing process—a sense of control. Each survivor's journey is their own, and I had to remind myself that my role was not to guide them toward what worked for me but to walk alongside them as they found what worked for them.

Operating in this intentional and trauma-informed way allowed me to create a space where both the survivor I was working with and my own survivorship could coexist. In those moments, I saw myself reflected in their courage, their struggles, and their resilience. I learned that healing is not a solitary act—it can be a shared experience, one that uplifts both the person seeking support and the person offering it.

This approach transformed how I connected with survivors. It helped me hold space for them without judgment or agenda, which in turn deepened my capacity for compassion. It also became an essential part of my own healing process. As I worked to support others, I found myself healing alongside them, acknowledging that while parts of me had been broken, they didn't define my ability to make an impact. Instead, they gave me insight, empathy, and the drive to create safe, affirming spaces for everyone in the room— including myself.

The agency I worked at had this concept of staff not disclosing their abuse. It was almost seen as one is not capable of doing the work if they disclose or speak freely about their abuse when working with others. I felt like I was working under the concept of the military's "*don't ask, don't tell*" policy. It was as though there was an added layer of shame put upon survivors who are professionals (mind you, this is completely opposite of how the movement started, with breaking the silence interrupting the shame). Instead, I saw this as an opportunity, when appropriate, to let survivors that I worked with know the benefits of counseling and that it is never too late to get help.

If I could share with survivors to give them hope on their path to healing, I felt it was my duty to help break the silence. I wish someone early on would have shared with me their journey to healing so that I could have witnessed what my future could have been a lot sooner. My diagnosis gave me the insight I needed to focus on what I could control. My PCL score was high.

The PCL (Posttraumatic Stress Disorder Checklist) is a standardized self-report questionnaire that my therapist used to assess the severity of my PTSD symptoms. My therapist explained to me over time, while working together, that we could lower my score. I could get to a place where my trauma is managed in a way that is healthy. Healthy!?!? Being healthy meant that I could be a better mom, wife, friend, and overall human. My diagnosis gave me something to focus on besides the trauma in itself.

My focus transitioned to healing. The thought of being a healed person scared me. I didn't know what that felt like. I finally told my husband about my brother abusing me and that I had other experiences in life that were similar, but the abuse at the hands of my brother greatly impacted me and how I showed up. I remember riding home from a night out with Shelley, one of my childhood friends, and telling her what happened. Reminding her of the time in junior high school when people would make fun of me for smelling and that was my way of protecting myself from my brother. Sharing my truth with people was a relief. It allowed me to breathe, and it took away some of the shame that I had associated with my experiences.

Everyone was not comfortable with me speaking freely about my trauma. I remember vividly around this time going out with some friends, and running into some of my brother's friends from the old neighborhood. They let me know that my brother (the abuser) was on his way up there. At this time, they didn't know that he was the last person I wanted to see. My friend/co-worker that I was with told her that I was ready to go. She could not understand why, especially since it was still early.

Disclosing at a nightclub did not just seem the appropriate thing to do. But she kept pressing me about why I wanted to leave, so I let her know that my brother, who sexually abused me growing up, was about to be here, and I didn't want to see him or engage with him. She looked at me and said we don't talk about things like this and basically not to bring it up because she doesn't talk about what happened with her brother. That night, I learned if someone wasn't comfortable with me disclosing my abuse that, 9 times out of 10, it had nothing to do with me and was more about their own trauma or lack of comfort. I learned that not everyone would be comfortable with me disclosing and talking about my abuse and that it was okay.

I found my tribe of people—my chosen family. These are individuals who are not just walking their own healing journeys but are also deeply invested in supporting others along the way. We hold each other accountable for our actions, celebrate each other's successes, and embrace failures as essential lessons on the path to growth. My tribe has become a safe space, a collective that nurtures authenticity, fosters connection, and provides the kind of support that is grounded in love and understanding.

This tribe is not just about showing up when times are good; they have been there for me during my darkest moments, offering encouragement, wisdom, and sometimes just a listening ear when I needed it most. The beautiful thing about this group is that the relationship is not one-sided. For the first time in my life, I have been able to show up for others in a way that feels healthy and affirming—not as a crutch or in a way that creates a negative trauma bond, but as someone who is genuinely invested in their well-being.

Our connection is rooted in mutual respect, shared values, and a collective commitment to growth. We have learned to give and receive grace, to have tough conversations when necessary and to stand in solidarity when life feels overwhelming. This balance has been transformative for me. It's taught me how to navigate relationships without falling into patterns of codependency or projecting my unhealed wounds onto others.

Having a tribe like this has been a crucial part of my healing journey. They remind me that I do not have to carry my burdens alone and that vulnerability is not a weakness but a strength. They have shown me the power of community—the kind that does not judge or criticize but instead uplifts and inspires. And in turn, I have learned how to be that person for them.

Through this tribe, I have experienced what it means to have relationships that are both emotionally safe and empowering. It's a stark contrast to the relationships I formed earlier in life, which were often driven by survival, control, or unhealed trauma. Now, I have a circle of people who truly see me—not just the version of me I have presented to the world but the real, raw, and evolving person that I am. And for that, I am forever grateful.

Thank you, Angela, Areial, Charlene, Courtney, Kelly, Shelley, Sherrie, and Tonae, for being a part of my tribe. I love ya'll!

Chapter Activity: The Survivor's Circle of Control: Reclaiming Your Power

This activity is designed to help you distinguish between what is within your control, what you can influence, and what is beyond your control. By shifting one's focus to what is manageable, one can regain a sense of agency in one's healing.

Step 1: Drawing Your Circles

On a sheet of paper or in a journal, draw three concentric circles and label them:

1. **Inner Circle – My Power (What I Can Control)**

   o These are the things that are entirely within your control.

   o Examples:

     ▪ Your healing journey and self-care practices

     ▪ The boundaries you set with others

     ▪ Who you allow in your life

     ▪ The words you speak to yourself (self-talk)

     ▪ Seeking support (therapy, support groups, journaling)

2. **Middle Circle – My Influence (What I Can Affect)**

   o These are things you may not control directly but can influence in some way.

   o Examples:

- Educating loved ones about trauma and healing

- Advocating for yourself in relationships or at work

- Participating in survivor advocacy efforts

- How you communicate your needs to others

3. **Outer Circle – Letting Go (What Is Outside My Control)**

   o These are things you do not have control over and need to release.

   o Examples:

      - The trauma that happened in the past

      - Other people's thoughts, actions, or opinions

      - Systemic barriers and injustices

      - Whether others choose to understand your experience

Step 2: Reflection and Action

- Look at your **Inner Circle**: Choose **one small action** you can take today to reclaim control over your healing. Write it down.

- Look at your **Middle Circle**: Identify **one area you can influence** and brainstorm how to approach it.

- Look at your **Outer Circle**: Pick **one thing to mentally release**—something you have been holding onto but cannot change. Close your eyes, take a deep breath, and visualize letting it go.

Step 3: Daily Practice

Each morning, revisit your **Inner Circle** and choose a small, manageable action to focus on for the day. At night, reflect:

- How did shifting my focus make me feel today?

- Did I notice any difference in my stress or emotional well-being?

- What will I focus on tomorrow?

Chapter 7
Forgiveness:
Reclaiming Power, Choosing Yourself

Forgiveness is a concept that carries weight, complexity, and often misconceptions. Defined simply, forgiveness is the process of letting go of resentment, bitterness, or the desire for retribution toward someone who has caused harm. The Bible speaks extensively about forgiveness, emphasizing its importance as a cornerstone of faith.

For instance, Matthew 6:14-15 teaches, *"For if you forgive other people when they sin against you, your heavenly Father will also forgive you. But if you do not forgive others of their sins, your Father will not forgive your sins."* Similarly, Ephesians 4:32 advises, *"Be kind and compassionate to one another, forgiving each other, just as in Christ God forgave you."*

While these teachings may resonate with many, they can feel suffocating or alienating to survivors of interpersonal trauma. Too often, survivors are told they **must** forgive their abuser, with the implication that their inability to do so is the obstacle to their healing. For me, hearing this directive was deeply disempowering. It made me feel invisible as if my pain and experiences were secondary to the absolution of those who had harmed me.

In those moments, I would disconnect. Sometimes, I froze, unable to process what I was hearing. Other times, I took flight, mentally or physically, leaving the conversation. What I heard in those moments wasn't a call to healing—it was a message that I didn't matter, that my healing was less important than the supposed redemption of my offenders. The narrative left no room for me to grieve, process, feel seen or believed, or choose myself.

The turning point for me was understanding that forgiveness is not about the abuser. It is not about excusing their actions, erasing the pain they caused, or extending them the grace they may not deserve. Forgiveness, as I have come to understand it, is about reclaiming power. It is about creating space for yourself to heal, to grow, and to move forward—on your own terms. Remember, my focus was to gain the power I needed to push through my trauma and move past being in constant survival mode.

Before I could even consider the idea of forgiving others, I had to start with forgiving myself. For years, I carried guilt, shame, and self-blame for things that were never my fault. I blamed myself for the ways I coped with my trauma as a child, as a teenager, and as an adult. But when I began to see myself not as the problem but as a person who had endured unimaginable pain. I realized that the first act of forgiveness I owed was to the little girl within me.

That little girl had suffered deeply. She had been sexually, mentally, and physically abused, and the domino effects of that trauma shaped her decision-making process for years. She fought with her mother—she carried the weight of guilt for adding stress to her mother, who was battling cancer. She entered relationships from a place of hurt, not love. She believed she was unworthy, unlovable, and not enough.

Forgiving her was not easy. It meant confronting the trauma I had buried. It meant acknowledging the years of coping mechanisms that had kept me alive but no longer served me. It meant holding space for both the hurt little girl and the resilient woman I had become. I forgave her for the fights, for the self-sabotage, for the years of believing lies about her worth. I forgave her for carrying shame that was never hers to bear. Most importantly, I forgave her for surviving the only way she knew how.

Forgiveness is not a one-time act; it's a process, a necessary part of my journey. Forgiving myself gave me the power to take control of my healing. It allowed me to see that my past actions, rooted in pain and survival, did not define who I am today. I am no longer that little girl, but I carry her with me. She needed healing before I could move forward; forgiving her was the key to unlocking that healing.

As survivors, we deserve the opportunity to choose ourselves without judgment. When forgiveness comes, it must be on our terms and for our benefit. It is not a demand anyone else can make of us. Forgiveness is a deeply personal act. For me, it began with acknowledging my pain, embracing my humanity, and deciding what mattered to me.

This chapter is not a call to forgive your abuser. If that does become part of your journey, that is okay. For no survivor's journey is the same. But it is a call to forgive yourself, to release the weight of guilt and shame that isn't yours to carry and to step into the fullness of your power. My healing did not happen in the shadow of someone else's redemption—it happened in the light of my own.

True transformation becomes possible when survivors are given the space to heal without the burden of others' expectations. And in that transformation, we find the strength not just to survive but to thrive.

You may be asking yourself, *"Did she ever forgive her brother or the others who caused her harm?"* The truth is, I have never spoken those words out loud or even internally—not in the way society traditionally defines forgiveness. For so long, I carried an intense desire for vengeance. I wanted them to feel a pain so excruciating that it could somehow match or even exceed what I had endured. It consumed me, becoming an anchor that kept me tied to my trauma in a negative way. But as I moved through my healing journey, I realized that holding on to that anger was only hurting me, not them.

Instead of obsessing over their punishment or wishing harm upon them, I began to let go of the grip they had on my mind and spirit. I stopped allowing them to occupy so much space in my thoughts. I stopped bringing them up in conversations, rehashing the pain with whoever would listen. Slowly, they became a non-factor in my life—a shadow of the past that no longer held power over my present or my future.

For me, this might very well be what forgiveness looks like. It was not about declaring, *"I forgive you,"* to them or anyone else. It was not about absolving them of their actions or pretending everything was okay. It was about releasing the hold they had on me and me, no longer wishing them harm. It was about reclaiming my energy, my thoughts, and my peace of mind. Forgiveness, for me, meant freeing myself from the prison of anger and resentment so I could move forward and truly live.

I have come to understand that forgiveness doesn't have to look the way we're often taught it should. It is not always about reconciliation, apologies, or dramatic declarations of closure. Forgiveness can manifest in subtle, powerful ways—like shifting your focus from the person who harmed you to the life you want to build. It can mean choosing not to carry the weight of their actions any longer or refusing to let their presence—or absence—define your self-worth.

For me, forgiveness was not about them; it was about me. It was a decision to prioritize my healing over my hatred. It was about breaking the cycle of pain, not for their benefit but for my own freedom. In doing so, I have come to understand that forgiveness, in whatever form it takes, is less about letting someone off the hook and more about letting yourself be free.

Chapter Activities: Forgiveness for Self

These activities are designed to help you reflect, process, and begin the journey of forgiving yourself. Take your time with each one, and remember to approach them with kindness and patience for yourself.

Activity 1: Write a Letter to Your Younger Self

1. Find a quiet, comfortable space where you can reflect without interruptions.

2. Imagine sitting across from your younger self at a time when they were experiencing pain or trauma.

3. Write a letter to them. Include:

    o Words of affirmation and encouragement.

    o An acknowledgment of their pain and their resilience.

    o Forgiveness for any choices or actions you may have judged harshly.

4. After completing the letter, read it aloud to yourself. If you feel comfortable, keep the letter in a special place to revisit as needed.

Activity 2: Create a Forgiveness Jar

1. Find a jar, box, or container that you can decorate or personalize.

2. Write down moments or thoughts for which you want to forgive yourself on small slips of paper. Examples could include:

   ○ "I forgive myself for believing I wasn't good enough."

   ○ "I forgive myself for my choices while trying to survive."

3. Place each slip in the jar as a symbolic act of release.

4. Whenever you feel burdened by guilt or shame, revisit the jar and remind yourself of the forgiveness you've extended to yourself.

Activity3: Build a Self-Forgiveness Affirmation Board

1. Gather materials such as paper, markers, magazines, or printed quotes.

2. Create a visual board that represents forgiveness and self-love. Include:

   ○ Affirmations like "I am enough" or "I forgive myself for my past."

   ○ Images or symbols that represent healing and growth.

   ○ Words or phrases that inspire you to let go of guilt and embrace your worth.

3. Display the board somewhere you can see it daily as a reminder of your journey toward forgiveness.

Chapter 8
Thriving through Post Traumatic Growth

As I continued my healing journey and deepened my work in the field of sexual assault and domestic violence, I stumbled upon a concept that felt like a revelation: post-traumatic growth. This idea was not new, but it wasn't something I heard discussed often—neither in my personal circles nor professionally. It became a way to reframe the trauma narrative and find a purpose beyond merely surviving.

Post-traumatic growth (PTG) is about more than resilience or bouncing back. It is the transformative process of using life's most devastating experiences as a catalyst for impactful change and higher psychological functioning. It's not about negating the pain or pretending it didn't happen but finding meaning in it—a way to create something meaningful from past experiences. It is the foundation for turning adversity into a deeper sense of purpose.

I could not control what happened to me. I could not rewrite the chapters of incest, rape, teen dating violence, or the systemic trauma that followed. But I could use those chapters to craft the rest of my story. In this part of my journey, I became keenly aware of how I could use what happened to me for systemic change in how we identify and respond to interpersonal violence and create spaces where survivors can thrive and lead.

When I decided to return to the rape crisis program, I knew this would not be just another job for me. It was a calling—a responsibility. I clearly envisioned how I wanted to show up in this space and the changes I needed to advocate for. During my conversations with the leadership of the program, I was upfront and unapologetic about my intentions and the perspective I would bring to the table.

I made it clear that returning meant embracing my truth as a survivor who had navigated many of the same systems we were working within. I would not shy away from centering the voices of survivors like me—those who had lived through trauma and systemic injustice. I was not just coming back as a professional; I was returning as a survivor leader.

Too often, I found myself in meetings where professionals were making decisions solely based on academic theory and research, disconnected from the realities of lived experiences and those most marginalized. These discussions often failed to consider the unique and complex needs of survivors.

Worse, the approaches being proposed sometimes caused more harm than good, only perpetuating the very cycles we were trying to break. I was committed to ensuring my perspective as a survivor leader was heard and valued. I knew that by speaking up, I could bridge the gap between theory and practice, bringing authenticity and real-world insight into spaces where it was sorely needed. My lived experiences gave me a lens that allowed me to see beyond the numbers and policies to the people—survivors who required more than a one-size-fits-all approach.

Survivors often experience secondary trauma when navigating systems or trying to access services, which is why I wanted to focus on systemic change. It was not enough to address individual survivors' needs in isolation.

I wanted to transform how we, as an agency, and the broader systems we worked within responded to survivors—especially those often overlooked or dismissed. Black women, in particular, have historically faced unique barriers to accessing justice, support, and healing. My mission was to challenge and dismantle those barriers.

Watching systems treat Black girls and women so differently when responding to their trauma was a painful reality to witness. Time and time again, I saw how racism and systemic inequities compounded the harm these survivors endured. It was not just about the trauma they had experienced—it was about how their pain was minimized, ignored, or invalidated by the very systems that were supposed to help them heal- thus creating a secondary trauma that often goes unaddressed as well.

Seeing this played out in real time made me question what some of my professional colleagues thought about me. Did they see me through the same lens of bias that shaped their responses to the survivors we served? Were there unconscious or even conscious biases influencing how they viewed my capabilities, my voice, and my worth? These questions lingered, but they did not paralyze me. Instead, I found strength in my mantra: *"You are safe."*

I repeated those words to myself at work, using them as a grounding tool. I refused to retreat into the trauma responses that had once consumed me—fight, flight, freeze, or fawn. Instead, I leaned into advocacy at a higher level, using my voice to call out inequities and demand change. I will continue to emphasize the need for holistic, survivor-centered approaches that are multifaceted.

1. **Individual Level:** Ensuring that every survivor, regardless of background, felt seen, heard, and believed. This meant providing culturally responsive, trauma-informed care that recognized the intersectionality of race, gender, and other identities.

2. **Interpersonal Level:** Create environments where survivors feel supported by their families, communities, and the professionals they encounter. Model empathy, compassion, consent, and safety.

3. **Institutional Level:** Advocating for policies and practices that address systemic inequities and prioritize the needs of marginalized survivors. This involved challenging outdated systems and pushing for meaningful reforms. It also includes training staff and partners to approach survivors with empathy and understanding of historical trauma, which is often one's present-day reality.

4. **Societal Level:** True transformation happens when we challenge deeply ingrained beliefs and structures that enable violence and silence survivors. This means actively shifting the narrative—through public awareness campaigns, media representation, and community conversations—to break down the stigma surrounding domestic violence and sexual abuse.

Standing Up for Survivors and Professionals

The disparities I saw in how systems treated Black girls and women did not exist in a vacuum. These same inequities extended to the treatment of Black and Brown women who worked within the anti-violence movement.

Many of my colleagues, including myself, experienced anti-Black racism and other forms of mistreatment while doing the work of supporting survivors. It was as if our voices were only valued when they served the narrative of the larger movement—one that often centered on whiteness and failed to acknowledge the unique challenges faced by women of color.

I could not stay silent. I began using my platform to advocate for both the survivors we served and the Black and Brown women working tirelessly within the movement. I worked to create access and opportunities for other Black women to step into leadership roles, knowing that representation matters.

When the statistics show that 60 percent of Black girls will experience sexual violence before the age of 18, it is clear that we need more Black women in leadership positions to ensure that prevention and response efforts are culturally responsive, effective, and inclusive.

Representation is not just about having faces that look like ours in positions of power—it is about creating systems that truly understand and respond to the lived realities of the communities they serve. Black girls and women face unique barriers to accessing care, support, and justice.

From the historical criminalization of Black girlhood to the stereotypes that paint us as angry, promiscuous, or unworthy of protection, the trauma we endure is compounded by systemic oppression.

To dismantle these barriers, we need leaders who can bring both professional expertise and lived experience to the table. Black women leaders are uniquely positioned to implement culturally responsive prevention and intervention strategies because they have lived the experiences they are working to address. They understand the nuances of what it means to survive in a world that often does not see your humanity.

Early on, I realized advocacy was not just about supporting survivors but also confronting systemic oppression and racism within the movement. Too often, I was the only Black person in the room, carrying the responsibility of addressing inequities for survivors of color, LGBTQ+ individuals, and other communities that were marginalized. As I rose in leadership, the microaggressions became more covert and harmful.

During a supervision session, a supervisor openly admitted to tokenizing me but failed to provide any concrete actions or commitments to stop this oppressive and racist practice. It was the audacity for me. Rather than acknowledging the harm and outlining steps for meaningful change, their admission remained an empty statement, reinforcing the very dynamics they claimed to recognize. The expectation to be both the voice and the solution for diversity efforts was exhausting.

Stepping into leadership roles as the first Black person or the only person of color came with immense challenges. The racial trauma I have endured—marked by isolation, scrutiny, and constant microaggressions—has been some of the most triggering moments of my career. From being tokenized without meaningful change to having my expertise questioned, I was forced to navigate spaces where my identity was both a barrier and a needed source for change.

The toll on my mental health was undeniable. The professional harm I experienced resurfaced childhood trauma, reigniting feelings of vulnerability. Recognizing the red flags, I sought therapy—not as a last resort, but as a form of self-preservation. Finding a Black woman counselor who understood my experiences without needing explanation was vital. Therapy became my anchor, helping me navigate racial trauma while maintaining my leadership.

The fight for equity in victim services is not just necessary but urgent. We must challenge the systems that perpetuate harm, not just for survivors but also for those doing the work. By amplifying Black and other marginalized voices, addressing systemic inequities, and centering healing, we can create a movement rooted in true justice and empowerment for *ALL* survivors.

It is time to disrupt the systems that perpetuate harm, both for the survivors we serve and for the professionals doing the work. The fight is not easy, but it is necessary. And I am committed to seeing it through. This is part of my purpose.

These experiences, while painful, are now part of my story. They have shaped me as a human. A professional and a survivor leader. These experiences of the last fifteen years deserve deeper exploration and will undoubtedly be the focus of another book. One that will explore the intersection of race and oppression in the nonprofit sector, particularly as it relates to the interpersonal violence movement and how we can make impactful change.

My work isn't just about supporting survivors—it's about dismantling systems of harm, both in society and within professional spaces. By addressing the challenges I have faced and the lessons I have learned, I hope to create pathways for other Black women leaders to thrive without facing the same barriers and harm.

Today, I have the privilege of leading a nonprofit in Northeast Ohio dedicated to supporting survivors of domestic violence, sexual assault, and human trafficking. As the first person of color to step into this role in the organization's 50-year history, I bring a deep commitment to fostering a trauma-informed, culturally responsive, and survivor-centered environment.

Today, I am privileged to work alongside leaders who are just as committed as I am to this work. They lead with heart, purpose, and a deep understanding of what's at stake. These are the people who fight for change even when it is hard, who show up for survivors with compassion, and who believe—like I do—that every survivor deserves to be seen, heard, and supported. Together, we're pushing systems to do better and building a future where healing and justice aren't just possible—they're expected. It is an honor to lead with them.

I am also the founder of **Inspiring Change, LLC**, a consulting firm dedicated to fostering transformative conversations that inspire individuals and organizations to flourish. A small business

I birthed out of wanting to train professionals in a manner that moved beyond theoretical knowledge into practical application for change.

With a specialized focus on diversity, equity, and inclusion, Inspiring Change empowers leaders to develop trauma-informed, inclusive organizations where all voices are valued and systemic inequities are dismantled. In 2025, I am launching the Rise & Lead program. Rise & Lead is an executive leadership cohort for women of color in the anti-violence field who seek to ascend to executive-level roles within the field.

Beyond my organizational leadership, I was a contributing author in the book *Sexual Assault Kits and Reforming the Response to Rape*, where I shared my expertise on improving equitable responses to all survivors with a focus on women of color. I am deeply passionate about training other professionals and equipping them with the tools and knowledge needed to respond effectively and compassionately to survivors.

My work extends nationally, where I have partnered with organizations such as the International Association of Chiefs of Police and RTI International Research Institute to improve the response to gender-based violence and advocate for equitable treatment of survivors of color.

At the University of Tennessee, I have collaborated with the Law Enforcement Innovation Center to develop and implement a cultural competency certification program for law enforcement. I have trained in over 25 states across the country. My mission is clear: to challenge harmful systems, disrupt inequities, and create a future where every survivor is met with culturally responsive and trauma-informed professionals, not barriers.

Today, I am thriving and using my journey to uplift others, inspire change, and pave the way for a more just and compassionate world.

I discovered a way to transform my trauma into something meaningful by using my experiences to help others, advocate, and create change. Through that process, I found my purpose. It did not happen overnight, and it certainly wasn't easy, but I refused to let my pain define me. Instead, I reclaimed my story and used it as a force for healing and empowerment. I now understand God's plan.

I challenge you to explore what healing looks like for you. Trauma can hold immense weight, but it does not have to control your narrative. Finding a way to shift its power through advocacy, creativity, connection, or personal growth. It can be a profound step toward reclaiming your life. Your path to healing is uniquely yours, but know that you are not alone in the journey. You have the strength to take back what was taken, rewrite your story, and step into your own power.

I know it is possible because I have done it myself. I have walked the difficult path of healing, reclaimed my power, and transformed my trauma into purpose. Over the years, I have had the privilege of witnessing so many other survivors do the same. For some, I was a small part of their journey—an honor forever embedded in my heart.

One thing I want you to take away from this book is this: You are more than what happened to you. Your trauma is part of your story, but it is not the whole story. You have the power to reclaim your life, to heal in your own way, and to step into the person you are meant to be. Healing is not about erasing the past; it is about learning to carry it differently—on your own terms, with your own strength.

You are not alone. You are not broken. And you are worthy of love, joy, and peace.

As you turn the final page, I hope you feel empowered to move forward—not just as a survivor but as someone who is thriving, growing, and embracing the fullness of life. Whatever your next step is, take it boldly. You deserve it.

Years ago, at a conference for victim advocates, I attended a writing workshop for survivors who worked in the field. I am ending this part of my journey by sharing with you the writing that sparked my survivor leadership.

I came here today because there was a new voice that I slowly recognized as my own. This voice was loud and clear.

It was then that I realized being out as a survivor was nothing to be ashamed of.

That I no longer needed to live up to other people's standards of who I should be as a mother, a friend, a daughter, a professional or even as a survivor.

This voice now cheers me on instead of stifling me.

This voice gives me purpose.

This voice is why I am here today.

One day, I asked God to use me as you see fit, for I am your soldier.

It was shortly after that I heard my voice say, loud and clear

"I was enough; job well done."

This is not the end of my story—it is the beginning of a new chapter. And if there is one thing I know for sure, I will continue to rise, lead, and fight for a world where survivors are empowered, not just to survive, but to lead and thrive.

Because we are not just survivors.

We are architects of change.

We are leaders.

And we are unstoppable.

www.ingramcontent.com/pod-product-compliance
Lightning Source LLC
Chambersburg PA
CBHW051216120626
46547CB00013B/1384